The Ancient Laugh of God

JUNE 22, 1998

FOR KAREN SADLON,

WHOSE SPIRITUAL LEADERSHIP
MEANS SO MUCH TO SHARON AND ME —
MAY YOU HEAR GOD'S
GRACIOUS LAUGHTER.

The Ancient Laugh of God

Divine Encounters in Unlikely Places

J. Marshall Jenkins

Westminster/John Knox Press
Louisville, Kentucky

Book design by Drew Stevens
Cover design by Drew Stevens
First edition

Published by Westminster/John Knox Press
Louisville, Kentucky

This book is printed on acid-free paper that meets the American National Standards Institute Z39.48 standard. ∞

PRINTED IN THE UNITED STATES OF AMERICA
9 8 7 6 5 4 3 2 1

Library of Congress Cataloging-in-Publication Data

Jenkins, J. Marshall, date.
    The ancient laugh of God : divine encounters in unlikely places /
J. Marshall Jenkins. — 1st ed.
        p.   cm.
    ISBN 0-664-25485-3 (alk. paper)
    1. Christian life—1960–   2. Irony.   I. Title.
BV4501.2.J433   1994
231.7—dc20   93-44314

In memory of my grandfather,
Rev. C. Rees Jenkins
1897–1993

Contents

Preface

Of any book about matters ancient or divine, the reader has a right to ask, indeed the reader should ask, What gives this author the authority to write about these things? Theology, after all, is intellectual hang gliding in which writer and reader sail at the mercy of the wind high above the rocks of their mortality. The reader needs assurance that the pilot, the writer, has credentials.

I have none. I am no saint, thank God. Never having attended seminary, I am not a pastor. My graduate background is in a field unrelated to ancient laughs of God, not to mention theology, and in fact many theologians view my discipline, counseling psychology, as an insidious parasite. I work as a counselor to college students, accommodating wisdom with the narcissism of youth and retaining much narcissism for myself in the process. I am an unlikely guide. Yet, I ask you to hang glide with me.

In each of these chapters, I search for Christ, sometimes calling him by name and sometimes not, sometimes searching scripture and sometimes searching peculiar places of experience and imagination. I never quite find him. I only catch glimpses, then he is gone. Like the disciples who walked with him unwittingly on the road to Emmaus, I am stunned to find that I recognize him in the breaking of bread as he vanishes from sight. I am left dumb, pale, my mouth agape, with only the realization that I did not find him but he found me, had me in his spell all along as I fretted over his absence and elusiveness. Then, if I listen closely, I can hear God's laughter in the heavens.

Each chapter, therefore, is a blurry snapshot, a fumbling attempt to capture and hold a glimpse of Christ in freeze-frame. The chapters are not systematically cemented to one another in a grand logical foundation for a thesis. Rather, they are held together loosely by an undercurrent of irony, the stuff of laughter and tears and wonder. The ironies discussed here come together in two thematic clusters: Part I consists of twelve chapters on the ironies of God's revelation in unlikely places, ways, and creatures. Part II consists of twelve chapters on the ironies of how a crucified Christ addresses our mortality with hope, how a suffering Christ answers our anxiety with eternity. The irony of incarnation holds both parts together. If writing this book did nothing else for me, it made me aware of the rich presence of the immortal Word in the mortal words of scripture, and it showed me how my mundane day-in-day-out world glows and groans in anticipation, pregnant with Christ.

Since this book derives from my faith journey, I must acknowledge those who nurture my living and writing. I dedicate the book to my grandfather, and in doing so, I thank my parents and all others who, like him, led me by example, often without knowing it. I appreciate Roland Tapp for encouraging me to share my writing with others, and I thank Kathy Gann and Nancy Case for helping me weather the clerical tedium necessary to do so. Although this book does not overtly address psychotherapeutic matters, it bears the mark of the suffering, healing, and hope that my clients honor me by sharing. It is also a product of Silver Creek Presbyterian Church, where dear friends allow me to share my writing, coloring my work with the love of my faith community. I also thank my friend and former pastor, Linda Woodard, who works quiet miracles of love in my life and the lives of so many others. And as I save the most precious for last, I thank my wife, Sharon, for sharing her courageous and caring life with me, and for her confidence in my writing that is much more steady than my own.

PART I

Ironies of Presence and Absence

But we have this treasure in earthen vessels, to show that the transcendent power belongs to God and not to us. We are afflicted in every way, but not crushed; perplexed, but not driven to despair; persecuted, but not forsaken; struck down, but not destroyed; always carrying in the body the death of Jesus, so that the life of Jesus may also be manifested in our bodies.

2 Corinthians 4:7–10, RSV

CHAPTER 1

The Ancient Laugh of God

> Then the LORD God formed man from the dust of the ground, and breathed into his nostrils the breath of life; and the man became a living being.
>
> *Genesis 2:7*

My wife and I live in a small apartment complex behind a dairy farm where no city lights or sounds disrupt the dark stillness of night. Soon after the sun sets we have stars, lots of stars. I wait until after nightfall to take out the garbage to a dumpster a hundred yards from our back door, and I tarry to and from the dumpster, my eyes on the stars.

A romantic about the night sky, I do not care to know about the phases of the stars, their density, or the chemical composition of their gases. But I do know that ancient people saw a cast of characters and configurations in the night sky: a bear, a dragon, seven sisters, a dipper held by a great unseen hand. I know that some of the starlight I see now has traveled so far that it was first emitted before my birth, some before this century, some, perhaps, before Christ. I know that the Milky Way consists of millions of stars the size of our sun or larger and that the seemingly small spaces between them make the distance between here and Pluto look like a mere walk to the dumpster. I know that some of the other flickers that I call stars are actually other teeming galaxies, some much greater than the Milky Way. In an infinite universe peppered with an untold number of solar systems, one can scarcely avoid imagining other planets peopled by children of God.

3

How might God's revelation take place on other planets? The possibilities are limitless. On one planet, God may choose to become visible, an infinitely expressive face in the heavens or a gentle giant lumbering about the planet and visiting each inhabitant at unforeseen but crucial moments. On another planet, the songs of angels may be heard echoing through the cosmos. On a third planet, where hurtling meteors and warp-speed starships blaze like lasers through the purple sky, infinite speed could disclose God as the great source of speed before a people who live for speed like we live for love or power. God may choose any means of revelation from as many ways as there are stars in the universe—and a hundred times more.

Here on Earth God spit on the dust and fingered a muddy blob, molding a man. But before drawing the breath to breathe life into this clay figure called Adam, God wondered how to reveal to this beloved little one, this human being of planet Earth, the Creator who formed him so tenderly. Pausing for a pensive moment, with eyebrows furrowed and lips pursed beneath a clay-caked finger, the Lord peered through a half-closed eye at this muddy form held in the hand that made him. Then a delighted twinkle sparked in that half-closed eye and a strange sadness crossed the other eye. Startled by a thought, God began to laugh, a low chuckle at first that built into a loud and hearty laugh as the Lord turned over the idea more and more. The laugh boomed so loud that the meteors hesitated, the angelic choir stammered, and the people of other planets scurried for cover. God laughed long and drenched Adam with tears, but that strange, pained sadness remained along with the delight in the Lord's eyes. Neither animal nor angel could be sure whether the torrent of divine tears came from joy or pain.

The crisp, still air outside my country apartment harbors no reverberating echoes from that ancient laugh, no sound from God. No face of God watches from the black, endless space among the stars. The headlines on the newspapers I just threw away tell of leaders fulfilling, at best, parts of their promises, making thin excuses for their errors in judgment, flexing their muscles at each other like boys in a schoolyard—no divine might there, no power of God. Ever since that great laugh, God has remained hidden and silent to the people of earth, and we sometimes wonder whether the Lord of heaven amounts to nothing more than a clever construction by some ancient astrologer, like the bear or dragon in the stars.

What was the great joke, the delightful irony that put God in stitches, the sad irony that left the Holy One silent and hidden for all this time? The irony was this: God chose to appear on planet Earth in the least likely places in order to reveal divine power through human weakness, holy love through mortal suffering, infinite greatness through the very smallness of this wet, muddy little one. The just and righteous God became known through Esau's good-for-nothing kid brother Jacob, who hoodwinked his blind father and ripped off his big brother's birthright, a birthright that would someday be called Israel, God's chosen nation. God, the faithful and mighty One, called a tongue-tied reclusive shepherd named Moses to lead a band of runaway slaves to God knows where, although they never quite knew whether they were coming or going. God, in steadfast faithfulness, gave these people their promised land and a king they adored, but God's wrath revealed itself through the barbarians who ran them out when their self-righteous complacency got to be too much. The voice of the Lord rang clearly through the prophet Isaiah (another tongue-tied one), commissioned to proclaim judgment to a people guaranteed not to listen.

God appeared through the birth of a baby in the donkey's quarters behind a cheap motel, through the life and teachings of a carpenter, through the persecution and execution of the Son of God at the hands of the highest religious and governmental authorities, through the drunken joy of his disciples who swore they saw a ghost.

On planet Earth, God chose to become known through weakness and folly—our weakness and folly—in places where we are least likely to look for evidence of a God of power and justice and mercy. Epiphany still happens where a child is afraid of things that go bump in the night, where a man gives a worn-out tennis racket to a boy, where a prisoner refuses to eat, where a rich man has everything and feels empty, where a single mother has nothing and feels fulfilled, where a college student longs to go home and dreads going home at the same time, where two strangers exchange a knowing look.

Look in the least likely places. Seek out the weakness and folly in the world around you and in your very soul. Those are the places of grace, the sanctuaries of God.

On a starry night I could take out the trash six times in the time it takes me to go once. The stars interest me, yes, but I really look past the stars, hoping against hope to see the face of the infinite God somewhere amid all that black infinity. Of course, it never appears. I go through the door of my apartment, to dirty dishes, to cats wrestling in front of a turned-on TV that nobody is watching, to my wife putting away a leftover casserole and wondering aloud when we will ever finish it, to the promise of more trash tomorrow night. This is a place of grace, a sanctuary of God. I can almost hear the laughter.

CHAPTER 2

The Word Became Flesh

> And the Word became flesh and lived among us, and we have seen his glory, the glory as of a father's only son, full of grace and truth.
>
> *John 1:14*

"In the beginning was the Word," John opens his great discourse on Christ, underscoring the terrible and creative power of words. We shape our world with words, imbuing with personal significance the things we name. In Georgia, we have one word for snow because it whitens our fields and closes our roads and delights our children and makes children of all of us only once in a cold blue moon. Eskimos have one hundred words for snow, it is said, because their world is snow. We call one another by name—Frank, Laura, Mr. Pettigrew, Miss Jones, Mrs. Stephens, Coach Kelly, Colonel Edwards, Dr. Talbert, sweetie pie, smarty-pants, conehead—and in the naming, in ascribing a word to a person, we create an identity for that person and a kind of relationship with that person. Words build walls that imprison entire nations, and they build bridges that set people free. Words break hearts and cure loneliness. Our creative powers issue forth in words, imposing our reason onto senselessness so that things make sense, bringing order to chaos, making something out of virtually nothing. When John speaks of the pre-existent Word that made all things, gave life to all living creatures and light to all people, he speaks of the mind of God issuing forth into chaos and making something out of literally nothing.

"In the beginning was the Word, and the Word was with God, and the Word was God. He was in the beginning with God. All things came into being through him, and without him not one thing came into being" (John 1:1–3). There are times and places too great for our words: A virgin forest. The ocean during a storm. A peak overlooking a great red canyon. The silence of the moon. Before such terrible beauties our words come to nothing, and we can only acknowledge in speechless silence that in the beginning was the Word, and through him all things were made.

We can say this too: The thing that makes these terrible beauties terrible is their indifference. Predators inhabit the thick green forest, beautiful beasts who would just as soon eat you or me for breakfast as they would any other hapless creature. The stormy sea that stirs our souls would wreck our vessel and suck us down. If we try to soar like an eagle in the great red canyon, the hard, barren ground below will have no mercy on our bones. The silence of the moon that never disturbs our prayers is the same silence that all too often answers them.

All creation groans under the weight of indifference to life, the very life that the Word brought into being in the act of creation. Life itself requires killing after killing: An owl swoops down and captures a squirrel. A fox ravages a goose. Bees and baboons and other communal creatures fight to the death for dominance. A human soldier shoots a human teenager. Nature's laws and ecological cycles continue undisturbed by human need: In San Francisco, the earth's crust shifts and settles like a god tossing in his sleep, collapsing roads and buildings, leaving thousands homeless or maimed or dead. Hurricane Hugo marches like Sherman through the Carolinas, wrecking a historic city, plundering the homes and property of entire communities, twisting and snapping great and ancient trees like twigs underfoot. Cancers, congenital diseases, strange viruses, addictions, and drunk drivers rob us of well-planned tomorrows.

Creation, that terrible beauty, seems to care only for

cycles of growth and decay, for survival of the fittest. The creative Word seems indifferent to our dreams, our wholeness, our basic need. After losing all he owned and his very children to bandits, fire, and storm, Job, the most righteous man in the land of Uz, sits in the stench of the city dump scratching his sores with a piece of a broken vase. "I cry to you," he pleads wearily to God, "and you do not answer me; I stand, and you merely look at me" (Job 30:20). We can conjure up our own words, construct poetic prayers and litigious arguments in an effort to persuade the creative Word to show us favor. We can back up our words with moral living, but in the end, we are reminded that in the beginning was the Word, not our words, and our words are helpless before this terrible beauty to influence our destinies.

In Ecclesiastes the preacher laments, "There is a vanity that takes place on earth, that there are righteous people who are treated according to the conduct of the wicked, and there are wicked people who are treated according to the conduct of the righteous. . . . The same fate comes to all, to the righteous and the wicked, to the good and the evil, to the clean and the unclean, to those who sacrifice and those who do not sacrifice" (Eccl. 8:14; 9:2). The shared fate, of course, is death.

"In him was life," John continues, "and the life was the light of all people. The light shines in the darkness, and the darkness did not overcome it" (John 1:4–5). Perhaps the darkness is the shadow of that terrible beauty, the creative Word, hovering in pure indifference over the planet. Or perhaps the darkness is our own confusion and despair when we find that our words do not pack the creative punch to overcome death and master our destinies. God knows we have tried. Our words have controlled plagues, devised high-powered computers, and taken us to the moon. But the terrible beauty of creation prevails again, leaving us in darkness no less deep, as the creations of our own words threaten to disperse our families, take over our will, or blow us to kingdom come.

Nevertheless, John is not speaking of the darkness, but of a light that the darkness of indifference or despair cannot understand or overcome. Could the creative Word be more than a terrible beauty, perfunctorily feeding us to the lions of fate? Might the Word seek intimacy with us, seek life with us above and beyond a lonely death according to nature's cycles? Watch the light, John answers. "The true light, which enlightens everyone, was coming into the world" (John 1:9), John sings for joy. The light piercing the dark night is no terrible beauty, but a ray as airy and silent and fragile as a dove.

The light illuminates a stable behind a cheap motel with a No Vacancy sign out front. Puffs from the nostrils of a cold, tired donkey whiten in the light. Perspiration glistens on the neck of a white-lipped man who just delivered his teenage wife's first baby in a bed of straw. Tears of pain and joy on the girl's cheeks flash in the light as she strokes the infant resting on her spent belly. The light shines on the raw red child, covered with a slimy film and wrapped in a tattered blanket, his eyes puffed shut, his tiny toothless mouth crying out like a lonely lamb as his mother strokes his delicate, wet temple with her finger.

"The Word became flesh," the evangelist writes with trembling fingers. The Word who "laid the foundation of the earth," who "shut in the sea with doors," who "commanded the morning," who knows "the way to the dwelling of light and . . . the place of darkness" (Job 38:1–21) cries out in this manger for milk and grasps his mother's earlobe. The Word became flesh: Nothing so contradictory can happen. But it has. The heavens should go up in flames, and the earth should collapse upon itself as the Word, the mind of God, must have surely gone mad to come forth as a gurgling infant. A thunderous, agonized roar of God should deafen every man, woman, and angel. But it is a silent night, a holy night. An infant coos.

"He was in the world, and the world came into being through him; yet the world did not know him" (John 1:10), because no one in their right mind would look in a

manger out back on a cold night for the Word of God
embodied on earth. "He came to what was his own," in
the form of one of his own, full of need and frightened by
the night, "and his own people did not accept him" (v. 11)
because, in the end, it is not the gulf between an indifferent Creator and a suffering human race that needs bridg-
ing, but the gulf between an indifferent humanity and a
loving, long-suffering Father. The child grows up and
makes a life of not being received, at best through our
misunderstanding, at worst through our rejection and
persecution of the Word made flesh, Jesus Christ.

The light shines beyond the manger, through thirty-
three years of dark nights, to a musty room where the
Word, the mind of God, stands in sandaled feet in an up-
per room with his disciples, bidding them farewell, asking
them to remember him. The light reflects in the wetness
in Jesus' eyes which nobody notices, and the light refracts
in a crimson ray from the wine he just poured. Judas's
drumming fingers make a shadow like a spider running.
Jesus knows that those who reject him will soon murder
him, and he has already forgiven them because he knows
that the Word made flesh is a contradiction too wonderful
for them to bear. He stands before his friends who do not
understand who he is, and rather than taking one last
shot at explaining himself, he simply offers himself in the
bread and wine and asks them to remember him. The
Word who fashioned the red canyon in his fingers, who
nurtured the redwood forest like grass, and who commanded the thunder to clap and the moon to be silent
stands before his friends with a lump in his throat and
asks that they remember him.

Jesus takes bread, breaks it, and gives it to his disciples,
saying, "This is my body, which is given for you. Do this in
remembrance of me" (Luke 22:19). It is as if he says, "This
is my body, the body of the Word who loved you before
you had bodies. This is my body, the body of the mind of
God, who gave teeth to the crocodile and color to the clouds
at sunset. Take, eat, for I come to overcome the indifference

in the universe and the indifference in your souls, to overcome death itself. Eat of this, my body, for from this day
forward, the creative Word of God will not be far away, but
will dwell within you and will love you more than you love
yourselves. Eat, in remembrance of me."

Jesus takes the cup, blesses it, and gives it to them,
saying, "This cup that is poured out for you is the new
covenant in my blood" (Luke 22:20). It is as if he says,
"This is my lifeblood, my life, the life that is the light of
all men and women, the life that danced and soared in the
far reaches of the heavens before I even thought to form
this planet. This is the life that I lose that your life will be
found. Drink in remembrance of me. Feed my lambs in
remembrance of me. Tell my story in remembrance of me.
Visit the prisoner and the infirm, clothe the naked, welcome the stranger in remembrance of me. It will not
change the world. Only I will change the world. Above
all, do the most humble, intimate act in remembrance of
me: eat, drink, together, and I will be with you in your
togetherness. I will be with you until the end of time
when all that will be left is the Word that was before
time—and something more. There will be you who remembered me, and we will eat and drink of Word and
life, and our joy will create a kingdom."

CHAPTER 3

Christ in the California Pizza Kitchen

> As he came out of the temple, one of his disciples said to
> him, "Look, Teacher, what large stones and what large
> buildings!" Then Jesus asked him, "Do you see these great
> buildings? Not one stone will be left here upon another; all
> will be thrown down."
>
> *Mark 13:1–2*

Recently I attended a three-day conference at the Westin
Lenox Hotel in Atlanta, adjacent to Lenox Square Shopping Mall. During a long lunch break one day, I reac-
quainted myself with the mall just to peek in a few shops
and especially to watch the people. The shops, the people,
the atmosphere at Lenox Square make me feel like a visitor on a strange planet. Perhaps the undying small-town
boy in me can never feel quite a part of the urban sophisti-
cation of the place. Maybe I feel curious about people who
shop for clothes that cost more than a car payment, or
about people who browse in map stores or gadget shops.
Or perhaps Lenox Square *is* another planet. Whatever the
case, the heart of the strangeness and wonder of Lenox
Square lies on the lower level, emitting the smells of
woodsmoke and cheese. It is the California Pizza Kitchen.

It has no walls, only a yellow diamond logo with the
silhouette of a palm tree in the middle. Everything is yellow, black, and white, but since the California Pizza
Kitchen scatters all over the first floor like an architectural
accident, the mall itself provides the decor: A bright orange Nintendo banner in the front of a video store. A rainbow of warm-up jackets through the window of Champs

Sporting Goods. Every mindful and mindless magazine
under the sun in an open newsstand. The Record Bar,
Tinder Box, and C. Dickens books. An AT&T Phone Store
with no phones in sight—only computer terminals. Escalators. An expansive high ceiling exposing an incredible
configuration of crossbeams and rafters as if to buttress
the very sky itself.

I find my way through the maze to a very tall, studious-
looking blonde woman who claims to be the hostess. She
seats me in the nonsmoking section and hands me a
menu. The restaurant specializes in wood-fired pizza, a
kind of smokehouse Italian delight with extraterrestrial
ingredients such as Maui onions, Jamaican banana chut-
ney, orange Peking sauce, spicy Tomato Yogurt Curry,
and grilled eggplant. The menu leads off with the Original
Barbecue Chicken Pizza, followed by such pizza delec-
tables as Chicken Burrito, Roasted Garlic Shrimp, Duck
Sausage, Thai Chicken, and Goat Cheese. Food for the
strange. I can't resist it.

A young Asian waitress with short hair, a headband,
and Buddha earrings appears from nowhere and asks
with a Southern accent what I would like to order. Erring
on the conventional side, I order the Five Cheese and Tomato Pizza with its fresh sliced tomatoes, basil leaves,
buffalo mozzarella, regular mozzarella, fontina, smoked
Gouda, and Romano cheeses. She disappears, and I join
the patrons who wait with varying degrees of patience. A
round woman wearing a large black hat and teal sweater
reads a music magazine. A delicate, nervous man with
bright-red, blow-dried hair, and a three-piece suit fever-
ishly puffs his cigarette. A pregnant lady in designer maternity clothes meets her husband for lunch. A college
couple who obviously have not dated long nervously work
on an appetizer, and two men somberly discuss the Dow,
the Super Bowl, and their failing marriages. A neatly
dressed gentleman in a tweed jacket over a light-blue
sweater sits alone.

Then it begins to dawn on me—why I feel like a visitor

on a strange planet here. It is a look in the eyes of the people gathered here for strange pizza as well as in the eyes of shoppers bustling about us—a distant, self-absorbed expression. Although there is no mirror in sight, I know that my eyes convey the same emptiness as if their faces mirror mine and mine theirs. We are ships passing in the night, and we know it. Perhaps only our hunger pangs bring us together in this place.

Of course the structure, the mall, also brings us together here in a quiet awe. If life does not impress us sufficiently, perhaps the escalators and colors and cross-beams and rafters and skylights do, reminding us that there are great things, if only those things made of mortar and steel. "Look, . . . what large stones and what large buildings!" we exclaim ever so silently, and even more silently Christ is here among us answering, "Do you see these great buildings? Not one stone will be left here upon another; all will be thrown down." Subliminally, at least, everyone hears his answer, the most deadly sound in the mall.

Christ is here among us in the California Pizza Kitchen waiting for his Chicken Sausage Pizza with homemade chicken sausage, Madeira-mustard sauce, spinach, and Italian parsley. Christ is here waiting for us as we have waited for him for two thousand years until the light of hope practically disappears from our eyes, until we place our hope in the hands of the mall merchants and wait impatiently for the instant gratification of a wood-fired pizza. Christ waits here today as he has waited since before time for us to open our eyes and really see one another, really see the Christ in one another, in one another's eyes.

Christ is here wearing Buddha earrings and smiling and taking our orders and wondering if today's tips will enable her to pay the rent. Christ hides under a large floppy black hat and behind a music magazine, afraid that someone will see her, afraid that someone will not. Christ, keyed up and working over a pack of cigarettes, his red hair like fire in a cloud of smoke, longs for peace when all the neon signs around him falsely proclaim, "Peace! Peace!" Christ is pregnant and worried that her husband no longer finds her attractive. Christ self-consciously shares appetizers with his date, prepared to die immediately if a piece of spinach gets trapped between his front teeth. Christ, imprisoned in the routine of the rat race, meets with a fellow prisoner for lunch. Christ sits alone and watches.

Christ is here in the California Pizza Kitchen. Christ is here in the waiting for pizza and in the delight when the waitress places the pizza before us. Christ is here in the eating pizza together and the longing to eat pizza together. Christ will remain here after the last Caribbean Shrimp, BLT, Shrimp Pesto, and Grilled Lime Chicken pizzas are served, after the California Pizza Kitchen goes up in woodsmoke, after time reduces Lenox Square to rubble excavated by architects one thousand years from now. It may take the tearing down of the mall walls and the buckling of the crossbeams and rafters to make us look into one another's eyes and finally see the Christ in our neighbor and in ourselves.

Meanwhile the pizza is served and my mouth waters. Slowly I eat, and if I lack the courage or the nerve to look into anyone's eyes while I eat, I at least give thanks for the eating and drinking, for the sending of God's only Son here in the eating and drinking. That is the least we can do—eat and drink, with our eyes open and watching for the Christ, the Lord who comes to us in strange places and stranger faces. In the eating and drinking and watching, we prepare ourselves to greet him when he comes to meet us in strange and wonderful places like the California Pizza Kitchen.

CHAPTER 4

The Invisibility of Christ

When Jesus had crossed again in the boat to the other side, a great crowd gathered around him. . . . Then one of the leaders of the synagogue named Jairus came and, when he saw him, fell at his feet and begged him repeatedly, "My little daughter is at the point of death. Come and lay your hands on her, so that she may be made well, and live." So he went with him.

And a large crowd followed him and pressed in on him. . . . When they came to the house of the leader of the synagogue, he saw a commotion, people weeping and wailing loudly. . . . Then he . . . went in where the child was. He took her by the hand and said . . . , "Little girl, get up!" And immediately the girl got up and began to walk about. . . . At this they were overcome with amazement. He strictly ordered them that no one should know this, and told them to give her something to eat.

He left that place and came to his hometown. . . . On the sabbath he began to teach in the synagogue, and many who heard him were astounded. They said, "Where did this man get all this? What is this wisdom that has been given to him? What deeds of power are being done by his hands! Is not this the carpenter, the son of Mary and brother of James and Joses and Judas and Simon, and are not his sisters here with us?" And they took offense at him.

Mark 5:21–24, 38, 40–6:3

Now on that same day two of them were going to a village called Emmaus, about seven miles from Jerusalem. . . .

17

While they were talking and discussing, Jesus himself came near and went with them, but their eyes were kept from recognizing him. And he said to them, "What are you discussing with each other while you walk along?" They stood still, looking sad. . . . They replied, "The things about Jesus of Nazareth, who was a prophet mighty in deed and word before God and all the people, and how our chief priests and leaders handed him over to be condemned to death and crucified him." . . .

As they came near the village to which they were going, he walked ahead as if he were going on. But they urged him strongly, saying, "Stay with us, because it is almost evening and the day is now nearly over." So he went in to stay with them. When he was at the table with them, he took bread, blessed and broke it, and gave it to them. Then their eyes were opened, and they recognized him; and he vanished from their sight.

Luke 24:13, 15–17, 19–20, 28–31

Invisibility never came easy for Jesus. Mark tells tales of sensational, show-stopping healings, only to have Jesus admonish the crowd to stifle their applause and pretend the show never came to town. Instead of just a miracle play, we have high comedy: An itinerant son of a carpenter from a someplace halfway between here and nowhere rambles into town, raises a young girl from the dead, and tells the local news media to shut off their cameras and go fetch her a Big Mac. "Don't mind me. I was just doing my job," Jesus seems to say with a tip of his hat as he rides off into the sunset with his twelve sidekicks. Of course, the cameras keep whirring—the show must go on—and the event is displayed and editorialized on the six o'clock news as word of the Galilean's magical medicine show spreads far and wide.

The laughter dies down, and comedy becomes tragedy as the tables turn and Jesus cannot make himself visible to save his life. He returns to the old hometown to teach in the synagogue, only to find that no one pays attention to his message. Everyone in town gets too caught up in seeing him for who they want him to be—just a hometown boy who ought to stay in line and build cabinets—rather than for the prophet and Son of God who he is. So he rides off into the sunset again, this time dejected, unable to convey his true purpose and identity to the people who matter most. This invisibility would eventually be the death of him, as the religious authorities in another town, never recognizing their long-awaited Messiah, would have him put to death.

The life of Jesus presents a tragicomic paradox: He was most visible while trying to stay behind the scenes and most invisible while trying to make himself and his message known. His healings cast into bold relief the first part of this paradox—his personal visibility while trying to keep himself out of the picture. When he performed a miraculous healing, Jesus wanted his patient and all witnesses to see the power of God's grace in action when it comes in contact with human faith. He did not want them to focus on Jesus and His Marvelous Galilean Medicine Show. He wanted them to focus on his merciful Father. He did not want them to miss the glory for the glitter, but the glitter entranced everyone, disciples included, until the final act when he returned from the dead.

Yet Jesus could not make himself recognized for who he was even when he rushed into the limelight and presented himself to those who longed the most to see him. According to Luke, Jesus' disciples almost did not recognize him when he returned from the dead. He was just another rolling stone on the road, short on information about the recent crucifixion but long on opinions. Then he broke bread with them and blessed it and started passing it around, and just as he disappeared into the woodwork, the disciples' eyes grew as big as saucers. They slapped their foreheads and cried, "It's you!" They clutched desperately into the thin air over his seat imploring, "Come back!" Then they settled back into their chairs, searching the room and the other sheet-white faces, tongue-tied somewhere between joy that he returned and agony that they just missed him. They had failed to recognize his face just as they had so often failed to hear what he said about his identity and destiny before the past week's nightmare.

What is the source of the problem? Why could nobody see Christ for who he was when it mattered most? Why could nobody see beyond Jesus to the Lord who sent him? Was Jesus just God's clown? Or was he the only sane person on a ship of fools? I believe the difficulty did not result from bungling on Jesus' part or from stupidity on the part of the disciples or crowds or Pharisees or Romans. Rather it resulted from the fact that we human beings seldom perceive what we have not preconceived, and the ways of the Father and the Son are far too marvelous for us to preconceive. In other words, we cannot see things that we can scarcely imagine, and we can scarcely imagine a Son of God.

Therefore, Jesus could not conceal the false self whom others preconceived, and he could not reveal the real self whom others could not imagine—his true, human and divine self. The hometown folk could only imagine him as "the carpenter, the son of Mary and brother of James and Joses and Judas and Simon," the kid who teased his sisters and played trombone in the high school band and wandered down the road and came back full of darned fool notions. Farther from home, people viewed him as an itinerant healer, a radical theological gadfly, a political long shot gaining a grass-roots following, or Elijah returned from the heavens—depending on the hopes and fears of Jesus' beholders. The visible Jesus was a media event, someone reporters would pigeonhole with catchy labels and sound bites, someone you might have seen on the news if you turned on the tube at the right time, someone you could turn off with the press of a button and write off as just another radical.

Jesus could reveal himself as anyone but the Christ, the Son of God. In a word, he could reveal himself as anyone but who he truly was. When he healed, witnesses marveled at the magical physician, not at the Messiah who offered glimpses of the merciful power, the kingdom, the face of God. When Jesus taught, he astonished people with his style, his authority, not with the Word setting his unsuspecting audience free. The people came for a show when they came to see Jesus, and even the critics who gave him rave reviews did not realize that they were watching the real thing, the salvation of their own souls from sin and death. Jesus was invisible because whenever he healed or taught, witnesses viewed a distorted image of him through faulty opera glasses of their own making.

Two thousand years later it seems as though we have seen it all. We have seen epidemics controlled, men walk on the moon, and uncanny special effects mailed to our hometowns from Hollywood and flashed onto the big screen. Each year, the media catalogs volumes of miracles, and the show goes on. This renders Jesus even more invisible. Jesus could scarcely grab our attention in the twentieth century with his miraculous words and deeds, not because he could not perform miracles but because we have grown accustomed to miracles. Miracles do not signify much. Science explains them away. We hold such sophisticated preconceptions about miracle workers that, were Jesus to cross our paths, we would explain him away on sight with our psychology or biochemistry or political science.

I suspect that Jesus dwells among us, sadder yet wiser for his past loneliness and frustrations. Here among us, flesh and blood, visible yet invisible, he is anonymous, a face in the crowd. Only unlike the rest of us, searching for identities and visibility through status or money or career achievement or miracles of our own, he accepts his invisibility with a sense of peace. It is the same peace he proclaimed but did not know quite as intimately two thousand years ago when it seemed so urgent to make himself and his message known. Now unburdened of the responsibility to make himself visible, he patiently waits for us to open our eyes and see him.

We can find him on a lonely road as we walk in days of grief or shattered hopes. He is a stranger, seemingly naïve, tired, ragged, hungry, another lost wanderer. Caught up in our own lives, we do not imagine that this stranger has a life of his own, his own trials and joys and memories. He walks with us anyway, accompanies us to a roadside diner, sits with us, breaks off a piece of bread and hands us the rest, and we look into his eyes for the first time.

CHAPTER 5

A Sign of Easter

At three o'clock Jesus cried out with a loud voice, . . . "My God, my God, why have you forsaken me?" . . . Then Jesus gave a loud cry and breathed his last. . . . Now when the centurion, who stood facing him, saw that in this way he breathed his last, he said, "Truly this man was God's Son!"

Mark 15:34, 37, 39

We are afflicted in every way, but not crushed; perplexed, but not driven to despair; persecuted, but not forsaken; struck down, but not destroyed; always carrying in the body the death of Jesus, so that the life of Jesus may also be made visible in our bodies.

2 Corinthians 4:8–10

I sit in a doctor's waiting room on a Tuesday morning, shifting in a hard chair, adapting my nose to the sterile, medicinal air, watching the clock. The doctor is thirty minutes late, and I am too involved in internal bickering to distract myself with a magazine. Time is money, I repeat to myself obsessively, and why should he have a monopoly on both? Will he prescribe hemorrhoid medicine for the wounds inflicted by endless waiting on this flea-market chair? Once he has billed me, will he engrave my name on his Jacuzzi to commemorate my financial contribution?

The bitter joy of my sarcastic rally is short-lived because out of the corner of my eye I see her: An obese, middle-aged woman with hot-pink rollers in her dry

23

brown hair watches me through thick, yellow, pointed
horn-rimmed glasses. She wears a pale-green dress with a
safety pin over her navel where once there was a button.
Her eyes alarm me, muddling my sarcastic preoccupa-
tions and replacing them with clear, raw dread. Those
eyes look miles away, set well over the horizon of her
fleshy cheekbones, but they project her simple, inevitable
will to begin talking when I give her the signal. And to
never stop.

The signal is eye contact, and no sooner am I filled with
dread than I stupidly signal my doom, reflexively looking
her in the eyes. Like a world-class sprinter, she starts out
of the blocks full force as soon as our eyes meet, talking
incessantly, scarcely pausing to draw a breath between
words, seldom permitting her shrill voice to waver. To her
credit, she gets to the point: her infinite ailments.

She stepped in a hole back in '77 while walking to the
drugstore to pick up her prescriptions and broke her ankle
in two places. Dr. Arnold Van Arsdale fixed it, so it seemed.
Then a few years later Dr. Liza Sanderkins X-rayed her for
a sore knee and found that the bones were set wrong. She
put her in the hospital—in her favorite room at that—
rebroke that ankle and reset it, but that didn't help a bit.
Then she took it to Dr. Joe Witherspoon, who said the problem was in her foot—tendon problems, probably stemming
from years of walking on the pavement to and from the
drugstore. He's been looking at it and squeezing it and
stretching it once every other week, and for some reason
her migraines aren't as bad on those weeks she sees Dr.
Witherspoon. But he says that bone and tendon problems,
especially in the foot, are going to heal slowly as long as
she is on that calcium-restricted diet Dr. Art Penney put
her on fifteen years ago. She can remember the first day
that kidney problem flared up. She was running around
like a crazy woman because she didn't know about her
thyroid condition yet, and on and on her medical history
goes. An entire order of monks would take decades of dili-
gent work to chronicle the whole thing.

Unable to listen to her words any longer, I listen to the sounds she emits like hundreds of caged birds at a zoo, a mechanical monotony of shrill sound, no more intended to communicate anything than the fidgeting of my backside in this stripped-down electric chair. She is as trapped in her own little world as I was in mine moments ago while ruminating over the sarcastic questions I will never have the courage to ask the doctor. The only difference between us is that she has hurled her world into mine, jolting me loose from my trivial obsessions, while I will never hope to free her from hers.

So, I conclude, we are two of a kind, she and I. The least I can do is listen, not to her words, mind you—there is nothing there—but to the sound of her voice. I attend to the look on her face, the way she holds her shoulders, the way she carries the safety pin over her navel. I look into her eyes again and continue listening, and in a moment, her eyes moisten a fraction of a drop more, her eyebrows hop, and her cheeks dance as, I suspect, it dawns on her that I actually may be listening. The jackhammer rhythm of her voice slowly subsides—no need for a jackhammer now because the wall between us is down. But the change in her is subtle, and not knowing what else to do, she continues talking about her aches and pains.

Not knowing what else to do, I continue silently listening to the tones, inflections, and rhythms of her speech, and I find, to my surprise, that I hear the sounds of her very heart. I hear a wistful love for simple things and a resignation in the face of a complex world. I hear a modest wish for companionship in a gaping pit of loneliness. I hear the force of a thousand joyful dreams from one who fears to awaken and give life to her dreams.

"My God, my God, why have you forsaken me?" I do not hear those words themselves so much as I hear hints of the tone, inflection, and rhythm of that cry in her speech. Nailed to a cross, trapped with a body of death, virtually resigned to her loneliness, she desperately speaks to make some tenuous connection with another person, hoping against hope for a sign of Easter in her speaking and my hearing. "Truly this one was God's Son!" a centurion's voice echoes from some long-forgotten place in my heart.

Her voice tone softens and her rhythm slows until, miraculously, we sit silently together with nothing more between us than the eye contact that started it all. I do not wish her good health; that is the last thing she needs to hear. Nor do I offer to help her in some way; I cannot or will not deliver. I merely thank her for sharing her story with me, and she responds with a half-touched, half-quizzical smile.

In my awkward thanks and her crooked smile, Easter somehow dawns. Great boulders are cast aside, and a kind of death is overcome in the communion of two unlikely saints. The silence of the waiting room becomes the silence of an empty tomb, and for the skip of a heartbeat, we share a sense of urgency as if something absurdly wonderful has happened that we must go and tell. But this is a doctor's waiting room, so we sit and wait, our eyes wandering from each other to our feet, to a table cluttered with magazines, to a clock, to a window. A door opens and a stout nurse calls, "Miss Brisson!" and she is gone.

CHAPTER 6

Brokenness and Blessedness

When Jesus saw the crowds, he went up the mountain; and after he sat down, his disciples came to him. Then he began to speak, and taught them, saying:

"Blessed are the poor in spirit, for theirs is the kingdom of heaven.

"Blessed are those who mourn, for they will be comforted.

"Blessed are the meek, for they will inherit the earth.

"Blessed are those who hunger and thirst for righteousness, for they will be filled.

"Blessed are the merciful, for they will receive mercy.

"Blessed are the pure in heart, for they will see God.

"Blessed are the peacemakers, for they will be called children of God.

"Blessed are those who are persecuted for righteousness' sake, for theirs is the kingdom of heaven.

"Blessed are you when people revile you and persecute you and utter all kinds of evil against you falsely on my account. Rejoice and be glad, for your reward is great in heaven, for in the same way they persecuted the prophets who were before you."

Matthew 5:1–12

A crowd waited on a hillside for Jesus. None of them knew quite what to expect, but they came because they heard rumors that Jesus had something to say that day. For Jesus, saying something usually amounted to doing something, doing something appalling or wonderful or mystifying. These people expected the unexpected.

Some came with the hope that Jesus would heal their deteriorating, aching, or maimed bodies. Others came with the hope that he would officially start his political campaign there, a rise to power that would win back Israel's integrity. Many wanted to find someone they could believe in, especially those who could not believe in themselves. Still others came for the show or the latest news story on this controversial Galilean, but even the curiosity seekers brought with them some sense of personal brokenness. All shared a longing to be blessed and made whole. Whether they admitted it or not, this longing was desperate enough to bring them to this remote place to meet this alleged savior—as unlikely a savior as he was unpredictable—and they hoped against all odds to hear their names called out and called blessed.

From atop the hill, Jesus watched the afternoon sun bathe the crowd with light. He saw the brokenness in their squinting and sweaty faces. This was not an IBM stockholders meeting or the audience at the Academy Awards. The irony struck Jesus as so rich that he could barely contain the impulse to laugh. These broken ones, these hapless and haggard ones were the most blessed of all precisely because their brokenness brought them where the beautiful people, the best and the brightest, would not show their faces. Jesus greeted them and tried to contain himself because no one could yet see that these pilgrims, who deemed themselves last, shall be first.

Jesus wondered how he should address these blessed ones who could not recognize their blessedness if you beat them over the head with it. Clouds crept toward them from the west, and thunder and rain disperse even those who believe that they deserve to be rained on. He only had time to tell them that in their brokenness they are blessed and in their blessedness they are still broken. He would tell them that, contrary to popular belief, they are the salt that gives flavor to this otherwise wasted planet. He would tell them that they are the light that reveals the splendor of the Lord, but he would also disclose how broken they are and how costly is their blessedness. He prayed quickly that they would not walk away as he said these things, but as he considered the suffering that comes with blessedness, he almost prayed that they would walk away after all.

With his disciples at his feet, Jesus stood and faced a crowd as green as the grassy hillside. They waited, unaware of who they were and who he was, unaware of the price they would pay to find themselves by giving themselves to him. Blessed are these green ones, he thought. Blessed are these whose blessedness is as silent and luminous as the stars. Blessed are these broken ones who are so perplexed in their sinfulness that they forget they have names, and blessed are these same broken ones who are so oppressed by the sinfulness of their world that they forget they have faces. Jesus wanted to say, "You have names. You have faces. In my God's kingdom, you are blessed with treasures that would be the envy of Solomon."

So he stepped up and said just that in so many words, in so many beatitudes, calling each of those gathered before him practically by name, depicting them as one who knew them since the beginning of time, promising their reward as someone who will stand with them at the end of time. "Blessed are the poor in spirit," he announced, hushing the crowd's murmur, "for theirs is the kingdom of heaven." So he began by greeting those who almost did not come, promising the hope of hopes and the dream of dreams to those who could scarcely admit that they could hope and dream so foolishly as to seek out this unlikely savior. Not only did the unlikeliness of Jesus fill them with doubt, but they almost did not come because of the unlikeliness of themselves, the unlikeliness that *they* could be blessed. If unbelief in a hidden, silent God did not sap their spirits, then unbelief that they were worthy of a loving God's love did.

In their coming and listening, Jesus saw that they believed, even if they did not know it themselves, and they hoped and dreamed that he would help their unbelief. So he blessed them, promising them a hope beyond their hopes and a dream beyond their dreams, not because of a saintliness that they could never attain, but because of the very sense of brokenness and spiritual poverty that made them wonder if they had the right to be there at all.

Looking more closely into their eyes, Jesus saw the face of a woman whose tears, like glaciers, carved rivers of grief into her cheeks since bandits murdered her husband. He saw the numb expression of a teenage prostitute who grieved the loss of her childhood and the angry eyes of a zealot who grieved the loss of his nation's integrity. "Blessed are those who mourn, for they will be comforted," he pronounced to a crowd that remained silent because his promise seemed too good to be true, although it was perhaps the assurance they most wanted. He addressed, in this blessing, the pain that brought these people to listen to a healer—the pain of losses that living incurs with every tick of the clock. The loss of youth and health, the loss of attachments and loves, the loss of hopes and dreams, the loss, perhaps, of faith itself brought each of them there just as loss and the anticipation of loss bring all of us to places where we hope to find, at the very least, comfort or, at the very most, Christ.

The crowd met his promise of comfort with silence because all of them learned as infants the hard lesson that one can cry out in pain and need, but one can only hope for temporary comfort. One can relieve pains and needs momentarily, but they return—if they are not always there. As they grew older, everyone there found pain and grief as inevitable as breathing and sleeping, and even with the most caring and comforting family or friends, pain and grief continue to come and linger and go in their own time.

Floods and fires and earthquakes fill the planet itself with pain and grief, and as the sun inched toward the cloudy west, every person in that crowd knew their grief was only an itch on a flea on a planet that was itself a

speck of dust in all creation. Every person gathered
on that hillside knew that if all of them cried out, if every
human on the planet wept aloud, the great silence of the
universe would go undisturbed. If the earth went up in
flames, the deep darkness of the universe would be no less
deep. If every life smothered like bacteria washed in alcohol, the groaning cycles and rhythms and movements of
the universe would continue in perfect indifference.
"Blessed are the meek, for they will inherit the earth," the
echo sounded as Jesus called his listeners great for knowing that they were small. He promised them, in their
smallness, a small planet, and he defied the vast and indifferent universe by blessing the people and the planet for
their smallness itself, and by declaring the obscure planet
their home if only because the Creator of the universe sent
him there.

It was an incredible promise, this guarantee that because of their smallness God would make this planet their
home. But perhaps more than the silence and indifference
of the universe, the silence and indifference of this
planet's supposed justice reminded them of their smallness. They could feel no belonging on this planet without
confidence that justice would uphold their right to be
here. Jesus surveyed the faces in the crowd and knew that
they would not have come if they expected any justice for
themselves on earth. If they expected justice, they would
not chase after and flock around healers or miracle workers like him, characters who promise to trick fate on their
behalf.

Jesus saw in their eyes raw hunger and thirst for a
home. They hungered and thirsted for justice, for righteousness' sake, because without justice and righteousness, this planet would not be worth inheriting. It would
not be home. "Blessed are those who hunger and thirst for
righteousness, for they will be filled," the hungry and
thirsty Christ cried out, blessing them and promising satisfaction not so much for their righteousness as for the
hunger and thirst that they shared with him.

A lump formed in Jesus' throat as he studied their
faces: An old man with bony cheeks and no teeth. A boy
with a furrowed brow. A mother with lonely, searching
eyes. A merchant with sleepy, skeptical eyes. A blind girl.
All gathered because of pain held in common, because of
brokenness in their bodies and souls. All of them, full of
confusion, doubt, grief, powerlessness, hunger, and thirst,
were sure to be healed, if not by a miracle, by their sense
of belonging there in that crowd with fellow sufferers.

"Blessed are the merciful, for they will receive mercy,"
Jesus proclaimed. It is as if he said, "Blessed are you who
listen to the poor in spirit and share their anguish and
perplexity with them. Blessed are you who give a shoul-
der to the bereaved and wet their hair with your tears and
share their grief with them as if it were your own. Blessed
are you who feel so touched by the smallness of the meek
that you become meek yourselves and show them their
beauty and their belonging. Blessed are you who get into
the skin of those who hunger and thirst for righteousness
until your hunger and thirst embodies righteousness itself. Blessed are all gathered here who share pain and
blessedness with your neighbor, for you will not stand
alone in your pain and blessedness. You will belong—you
do belong—together."

A woman batted gnats swarming about her face. A tall,
muscular farmer reclined. All eyes focused on Jesus, all
ears listened intently. If it was not the strange joy of his
greeting then it was the strange hope of their coming to
that place that opened their eyes and attuned their ears
and cleared their heads. In all but a few waking moments
of our lives, we have at least three things on our minds at
once. We seldom ask for anything for the stated reason
alone, seldom give anything without the hunch that there
is something in it for us. But in this lucid, uncluttered
moment, Jesus spoke in unadulterated love for his hear-
ers, and all who gathered soon forgot the need that
brought them there and listened for the sake of the one
who spoke. "Blessed are the pure in heart," Jesus pro-

claimed, sensing that they might never be more pure in heart than they were at that moment as their wide-open eyes revealed that he was growing bigger than life to them. "For they will see God," he concluded as they wondered in their pure and secret hearts whether it was God whom they saw and heard from the hilltop.

The voice of Jesus echoed in the valley and faded away, leaving a silence as rich as their purified hearts. This was peace, if only for a moment, the peace of simply being together, brought there by the pain wrought by the world's violence, united by hope and mercy, made one by a single-minded, pure-hearted focus on a fellow sufferer calling them blessed for their suffering and brokenness. This was peace, a silent moment of communion amid a truth that, brilliant as the sun, one could only behold for an instant. The silence would break in a while, with every heart cluttering up with the contradictory needs and pursuits of living. The silence would fade into the sounds of voices and hammers, of wind and fire. But in another sense, the silence would never break, the peace of this moment would never pass for those gathered here who would re-create it by building bridges between broken people in the full light of this moment's truth. "Blessed are the peacemakers, for they will be called children of God," Jesus broke the silence, startling himself with the violent implications of this blessing.

Children of God sustain the peace of this moment by building right relationships, but they also suffer in a world that hates peacemaking. This moment of peace on the hillside, with all hearts focused on the one truth of God, with all souls bonded by common brokenness and blessedness—this moment was the kingdom of heaven manifested here on earth. This peace, this kingdom scandalizes all who maintain power by the division of their subjects against one another. The powerful persecute children of God for hungering and thirsting for right relationships, for building peace that trivializes power. That ugly truth would lead to the murder of Jesus and the persecution of the broken and pure ones who listened to him that day.

"Blessed are those who are persecuted for righteousness' sake, for theirs is the kingdom of heaven," Jesus cried out with a cracking voice, promising that they could seize this moment of peace again after the violence ends, promising them the same kingdom of heaven which he promised to the poor in spirit. To those who would suffer for building right relationships between people in spite of human brokenness, Jesus promised the same kingdom of heaven that he promised to those who sought a right relationship with God in spite of themselves. But he wanted to make sure they understood the violence they would go through before this moment of peace would become eternity. "Blessed are you when people revile you and persecute you and utter all kinds of evil against you falsely on my account. Rejoice and be glad, for your reward is great in heaven, for in the same way they persecuted the prophets who were before you."

Now it was weeping that he fought back, weeping not only for the persecution they would endure for his sake, but for the fact that they were still there. Listening. Wide-eyed. Green. Jesus took a deep breath. Blessed are these green ones, he thought, for theirs is the kingdom of heaven as surely as this moment together is the kingdom of heaven. He looked up and saw the clouds rolling in from the west. There was more terrible and lovely truth to tell, more to share of the kingdom. He swallowed hard and continued to teach before they would indeed go their separate ways.

CHAPTER 7

History and Futility

Indeed, God did not send the Son into the world to condemn the world, but in order that the world might be
saved through him.

John 3:17

We think of history in terms of human actions: A pharaoh
decides that he needs some slaves. An old black woman
drinks from a fountain beneath a For Whites Only sign. A
Lebanese mother calls for her children. A night watchman sees glowing flickers on the horizon. A space traveler's family watches the craft explode before it can exit
the atmosphere.

History consists of human beings like the ocean consists of drops of water or the desert, grains of sand. Some
people spend more time in the limelight than others, and
some make decisions that shake the foundations of millions of human homes, but by and large we all play bit
parts in an expansive, seemingly endless drama. Yet we
are also the stuff that history is made of, so history is as
human as a lover's blush, an off-color joke, or the tears of
an old man in an empty room.

History engulfs us like the sea engulfs a sea horse, and
like the sea horse and its sea, we are so immersed in our
history that we scarcely recognize it from day to day. But
unlike the sea horse, it occasionally dawns on us that
days have passed and we have changed, so history must
have happened. Thus we anxiously appoint some of the
more articulate and observant members of our species to

record our memories of ourselves and our days. We call these articulate observers historians.

Historians have been at work for a long time, so long, in fact, that some historians write histories of historians. Universities spend millions of dollars for libraries that house history books. But all too often we honor and preserve the work of historians in order to cling to the familiar past as we slide backward into the unfamiliar future; meanwhile, the historians themselves would have us learn from the past in order to face tomorrow squarely. Perhaps the greatest upshot of history is that we do not allow ourselves to learn much from history, that we tend to repeat follies and sins that we read and moralized about in grade school. Although eager to pickle our past for later consumption, for now we must tilt at tomorrow's windmills.

Few historians' versions of history speak kindly of the humans who make history. No "great" men or women were not at least half baked, and most "great" discoveries or revolutions or turning points seem to have occurred as much because their time had come as because some bold or ingenious humans engineered them. The human spirit has been greatest among the weakest, as when the ancient Israelites escaped captivity or when the black citizens of Montgomery boycotted the buses. But if the last shall be first and the first last, history seems like an endless cycle of the last rising bravely to the top and falling over and over again.

Since most of us at least fancy ourselves to be moral people, the seeming futility of human history should confound or offend anyone who takes the morality of our actions seriously. Moral action presupposes that moral purpose is woven into the warp and woof of the human community and its history. But those who truly take the morality of their actions seriously find themselves the most vulnerable people of all to a sickening sense of moral futility. The serious moral agent juggles too many dilemmas: "How can I care about the economy when the bulk of the nation's wealth lands in the bank accounts of the wealthiest few? How can I depend upon rights when legal outcomes depend primarily on who has the craftier attorney? Shall I compensate victims of injustice at the risk of weakening their resolve to fight for themselves? Or shall I help empower them to overcome oppression at the risk of encouraging them to become oppressors themselves?

"Surely God must be above this mess, this sweaty, moody, redundant, exasperating human thing called 'history.' Surely my smallness and moral befuddlement must result from my brokenness, my estrangement from God, my descent from Adam. Surely God must look down on this tragic circus paralyzed with indecision over whether to laugh or cry."

From such a desperate perspective, perhaps the serious moral agent could not find a role for God in history without seeing all moral plans and schemes as rituals of praise and honor, like the offering of lambs at a flaming altar. Our moral acts might boil down to aesthetic acts like the dance of dancers in a royal court or the little drummer boy's playing for the baby Jesus. The moral act may have no ultimate utility at all beyond its beauty and integrity or beyond the way it touches the heart of a spectator God. Our moral acts may amount to little more than Abel's offering of meat and Cain's offering of vegetables, valued according to the fancies of the divine palate. God, then, would stand above this human mess in detached self-contemplation like Aristotle's god; or God, like the divine clockmaker of the Deists, could set the hands of time and enjoy a good smoke while watching human history tick away.

God, however, chose not to be above this mess. God came as an infant son one cold night in a hick town called Bethlehem amid the smells of dung and straw, the sounds of his mother's moans and screams echoing in the blurry stars, the sight of his father's tense, perspiring face. God came drenched in blood and slime, crying for the warmth and calming darkness of the womb, his father cutting and tying his umbilical cord. An infant so helpless he would die if left alone, so weak he could not hold up his eggshell head, he clung to his mother's breast.

Jesus would become one of the anonymous, disenfranchised people traipsing into the wilderness to be baptized by a madman. He would be seen again through the dust rising on the road, kissing lepers, chastising holy men, seeking out lonely places. He would hurry from town to town with an urgent message of a kingdom that even his disciples could not understand. In his life there was much to do and little time. There was much walking and teaching and weeping. Seldom did he see a face that did not betray a hidden anguish or confusion or fury. He came, a misunderstood, rambling rabbi in a world, in a human history that cried out and cries out still for a savior. He came, that savior, into a history so full of futility that the human beings he came to save killed him.

Before we humans killed him, he commanded that we love God and love one another, as if perhaps history had some point, some purpose after all. He commanded that we act morally because a kingdom is coming, not a utopia that our moral acts would bring into being, but a kingdom brought by God in which the true purpose of our moral actions would become clear in him. Also he commanded that we wait—wait together in his name for him to come again and again until his final coming in human history, foreshadowed by his resurrection from death.

His coming once means that we encounter him in a grieving widow, an angry street gang leader, a lonely man with AIDS, a forgotten child, and he commanded that we open our eyes and see his wounded face and reach out with compassion. His coming twice means that we encounter him in the birth of a child, a girl with Down's syndrome singing "Happy Birthday," the hope and fortitude of a young black woman in South Africa, the hymn of a prisoner, and he commands that we open our eyes and see him in his beauty and lift up a song of praise. All the while we wait together for his final coming, foreshadowed in his coming once in suffering and twice in hope, the final coming that takes human history in all its futility and fulfills it, the coming that takes the human beings who constitute history and makes us whole.

CHAPTER 8

Aliens

Beloved, I urge you as aliens and exiles to abstain from the desires of the flesh that wage war against the soul. Conduct yourselves honorably among the Gentiles, so that, though they malign you as evildoers, they may see your honorable deeds and glorify God when he comes to judge.

1 Peter 2:11–12

In a scene from the movie *E.T.*, a boy with a flashlight tracked unearthly footprints through the brush in a vacant lot one night, parted high weeds with his free hand, and encountered nose to nose a green, cow-eyed, naked freak with a wide, flat head, a potbelly, a fluttering, fluorescent heart, and enormous feet, screeching and fleeing at the sight of a frightened Earth boy.

Jonathan Swift's Gulliver awakened on shore after a shipwreck, captive to an entire colony of people six inches tall.

In the movie *The Gods Must Be Crazy,* an African bushman, innocent and naked as the day he was born, retrieved a Coke bottle thrown from a plane. Seeking to return the bottle to the gods, he wandered far from his tribe and into the clutches of civilization, where neither he nor the white people knew what to do with each other.

A quarter of a century ago, our black-and-white TV screens glowed with the image of Uncle Martin on "My Favorite Martian," who looked and sounded like any other gentleman except that he faced life's little problems by projecting two antennae from the back of his head with which he transmitted novel solutions from Mars.

More recently, on the evening news, our color TVs glowed with desperate, hungry Mexican faces, smuggled illegally into the United States to work the fields for wages lower than any American citizen would accept.

E.T., Gulliver, a bushman in the city, Uncle Martin, the Mexican farmworker in Texas have little in common, but they have one thing in common that makes all the difference: They are aliens. Not because they look different from us: Only E.T. looked appreciably different. Not because they talk different from us: Gulliver and Uncle Martin spoke fluent English, and E.T. picked up a few words rather easily. They are not aliens because they differ from us at all. Any of us would be aliens if displaced on another planet or in another country or in another world. Aliens are not aliens because of who they are but because of where they are: Someplace that is not home. But they are not merely homeless. Aliens are defined not only by being in a place that is not home but also by *having a home* far away, a home that they long for and dream of. E.T. was an alien not only because he was an inadvertent exile on the wrong planet but because he longed—he lived—to phone home.

Peter identified for us another group of aliens: ourselves. "Beloved . . . aliens and exiles," Peter greeted the early church and you and me. In Peter's age he and his beloved friends in the church were obvious aliens, displaced far from home like innocent natives in a cold, complex city. Peter wrote his warm greeting from Rome, practically the world capital, and all the ways of the world, all the world's policies, priorities, and purposes started there. The Roman government supported their policies, priorities, and purposes with golden gods for the people to worship, gods who accommodated themselves to the wishes of the emperor or the workings of the status quo. Furthermore, the Romans could transport these domesticated, manageable gods to places where they better served the emperor's purpose, or they could melt them down and remold new and improved gods. Any law-abiding citizen who wanted to be left alone needed only to make an occasional gesture of deference to the gods.

The Christians, however, would never make things easy for themselves, would never make themselves at home because they refused to acknowledge the Roman gods. The Christians were aliens displaced from another reality altogether because their one, invisible God conformed to no emperor's whims. This God had a totally free, untouchable will. Unable to attack the invisible, undomesticated, unmanageable God of the Christians, the Romans attacked God's alien children, the Christians themselves. The Romans distorted the meaning of the Lord's Supper and accused the Christians of cannibalism. They took a cheap and narrow view of the Christians' obedience to an unmanageable, invisible God, branding the Christians atheists. Nero made the Christians scapegoats for his own failings, feeding them to the lions because they were aliens, exiles, and easy prey.

Christians could not call such a hostile environment their home. But they had a home, and they knew the comfort and joy of their home. In their home, the Roman gods were just pieces of furniture, and the God of the Christians, so wild and unruly to the Romans, was faithful and steadfast. Jesus called his home the kingdom of God, and he promised it to the Christians. He made good on his promise, dying the death that we started with our sin and rising again with the life that God started with love. So the Christians faced Nero's lions with a strange and alien smile, knowing that death itself could not stand in the way of their going home.

Much has changed in the two thousand years since the emperor Nero reigned. Rome no longer rules the world, and here in America's churches, we worship as Christians, unbothered by the powers that be. In fact, many of the powers that be worship in scattered churches throughout the nation, continuing an unlikely marriage of Christianity and political power started by the emperor Constantine before the Roman Empire fell. Since then,

Christians conquered and baptized entire nations, and when defeated, they often converted their conquerors. Today in much of America, Christendom is status quo, and those who do not profess the Christian faith are aliens in a nominal sense.

In a more real sense, very little has changed. We worship the same unshackled, unaccommodating, invisible God who irritated the ancient Romans, and when taken seriously, this God can be just as unshackled and unaccommodating to the cultural and political powers that be two thousand years later. We are aliens because even if we are Republicans or Democrats, Presbyterians or Pentecostals, hawks or doves, we worship a God who defies labels and pronounces, "I AM WHO I AM" (Ex. 3:14). We are aliens because even if we work fifty or sixty hours a week managing investments, we worship a God who cares more about a homeless woman getting a bowl of soup than about the Dow-Jones industrial average. We are aliens because even if we give our labor and taxes to powers that be who manage us economically and politically, we give our lives to a God who sets our spirits free. We are aliens because even if we work toward the technological control of nature, we trust in a God who controlled nature before we ever existed.

Above all, we are aliens because even if we have a home with a spouse, two kids, and a white picket fence, we gaze into the dark night and pray to our caring, liberating, mysterious God to take us to another home prepared for us. That remains the essence of being an alien—longing for a home. Over two thousand years of our history, we Christians have been freaky visitors, innocent natives in a brutal city, inconspicuous citizens with an offbeat faith, or exiles searching for a place to just start over with life. Such aliens usually blend in or become extinct. But we remain viable aliens because if death itself cannot break Christ's promise of the kingdom, the passing of two thousand years cannot break the promise of a home.

Of course, Christ himself was an alien, and although he

created this earth, he remains here as a stranger. So as aliens, we carry on his legacy, and he makes his presence known to those who greet strangers such as ourselves. But because he created this world, and because he still lives, an alien in and among us, we are never too far from home.

Aliens often do go home. After a chase scene that included flying bicycles and hijacking a government truck, the Earth boy and E.T. tenderly touched forefingers. E.T. said "Ouch," the only word he knew for feeling, and boarded the rescue starship. Gulliver sailed to England. The African bushman ambled back through the wilds to his native settlement, where his children rushed to greet him. I suppose Uncle Martin blended in so well with the earthlings that he made suburban America his home, and I hope that the Mexican farmworker found the means to live with loved ones.

Even at this very moment, there is another way for aliens to go home. Alien Christians come together, bow their heads, and pray in the name of Christ, whose presence makes every prayer, every mention of his name by those who love him, a homecoming.

CHAPTER 9

The Wildfire

The voice of the LORD is over the waters;
    the God of glory thunders,
    the LORD, over mighty waters.
The voice of the LORD is powerful;
    the voice of the LORD is full of majesty.

The voice of the LORD breaks the cedars;
    the LORD breaks the cedars of Lebanon.
He makes Lebanon skip like a calf,
    and Sirion like a young wild ox.

The voice of the LORD flashes forth flames of fire.
The voice of the LORD shakes the wilderness;
    the LORD shakes the wilderness of Kadesh.

The voice of the LORD causes the oaks to whirl,
    and strips the forest bare;
    and in his temple all say, "Glory!"
Psalm 29:3–9

When the day of Pentecost had come, they were all to-gether in one place. And suddenly from heaven there came a sound like the rush of a violent wind, and it filled the entire house where they were sitting. Divided tongues, as of fire, appeared among them, and a tongue rested on each of them. All of them were filled with the Holy Spirit and began to speak in other languages, as the Spirit gave them ability.

Acts 2:1–4

One cloudy evening in a forest, the darkness runs so thick and deep that even the creatures of the night consign themselves to blindness. No moon or stars light the sky. The smells of unfallen rain and virgin wood fill the forest. The wind moans in unseen trees.

Then a blinding white rip reports like a thousand cannons firing at once, rending the veil of night from top to bottom. For an instant of an instant, whiteness floods the forest, exposing sketchy outlines of every plant and animal and rock and crevice. The lightning bolt strikes a tall tree, corkscrews to the trunk, and projects at eye level into the woods, ricocheting from tree to tree, scattering bark and splinters and stunned, hurtling branches.

Millions of glowing red sparks climb upward and drift outward in the black night. As the stricken tree falls, it lights up like a torch and crashes into more trees as millions upon millions more red sparks fill the night. Flames dance for joy on the fallen tree and spritely leap to neighboring trees. Sparks light on leaves and twigs, and everywhere tiny flames are born dancing, then whipped into dancing athletes and then into dancing titans leaping from tree to tree. All animals scurry or sprint or burrow in a frantic search for the deep, cool darkness of a moment before. The crackling, banging sounds of burning wood are overtaken by the coursing moan of the rushing flames. All the wood is ablaze with trees falling and flames towering into the pale, glowing sky from which the fire first descended.

Pentecost was like that fire. Jesus rived the spiritual night of Israel like lightning, healing lepers and giving sight to the blind, overturning and scattering the religious order with his blessings for sinners and curses for the self-righteous, cleansing the Temple and facing his absurd death like a task to be done. The curtain of the Temple was torn from top to bottom, his disciples nervously scurrying in the shadows. There was cursing and spitting and gambling and laughing and rain and darkness. There was stunned silence. Then Mary Magdalene stood confused in an empty tomb, and there was more running and shouting. Bewildered Roman guards and Roman officials and high priests paced and muttered about resurrection rumors stirring the people. There was a stranger on a road, a breaking of bread, the face of Christ, life itself eternal.

Sparks flew everywhere about this towering light, this Christ. They ignited Peter and the disciples and all who were around them. There was speaking in tongues. There was preaching and teaching and healing and walking the roads of Jerusalem, then of Israel, then of the whole empire and of the whole world. Persecution became deliverance, and a persecutor became an apostle. People rallied about the story of a suffering servant, a hunted, executed Galilean who lives. Churches were born, armed against a hostile world with the strange power of their suffering and the madness of their hope, faith, and love. The flames spread and rose and endured even as the Roman Empire fell.

Back to the blazing forest. An insomniac in the nearest town glances out his window and sees a glow in the distant sky. Pressing his face against the glass, he sees that the glow emanates from a more intensely glowing source in the forest. He rushes to the phone, dials 911, and notifies the operator.

Soon firefighters in helicopters hover in the sky, and others in jeeps and trucks and on foot swarm the roads and trails, penetrating the forest. Chain saws whine and trees fall to stop the march of flames leading toward town. Shovels pound into the ground like pistons as men dig ditches, smoke stinging their sweaty faces. Water gushes from the sky and from the ground, filling new ditches, saturating old trees.

All through the night and through the day and into the next night they work, never noticing the anxious racing of their hearts. You can't bridle and break fire like you can a horse. You can't cage it like a bear. You certainly can't make it reasonable like a growing child. You can't make it speak your language, can't make it speak at all. It has a will only to march and grow and consume. Fire is no respecter of persons. It would just as soon burn a human as a tree. So humans fear fire, and the only way they know to control it is to kill it.

People fear the Holy Spirit, the Pentecost Fire, in the same way. Bystanders at the Pentecost tried to explain it away, calling the ecstatic disciples and other faithful a bunch of drunkards. They started a long tradition of efforts to explain the Spirit away, from ancient Romans calling Christians atheists for worshiping an invisible God to modern Freudians calling Christians wishful thinkers who long for a father figure. Other onlookers, the ones with swords, would try to control the Fire with persecution, throwing Christians to hungry lions or hanging them from more trees. But it is hard to douse a flame kindled in persecution by persecuting more people, and eventually the Fire lit on the persecutors themselves.

Perhaps the ones most frightened by the Fire were the ones who were also most filled with joy—the flaming Christians—and they had the most success at controlling it. Once the ecstasy of Pentecost passed, they saw the flames raging on in the church and in their own souls, and many feared what the Fire might ultimately do. Some sought to control it by understanding it, and theology was born. They quibbled over whether Jesus was begotten or made, whether soul and body are separate or one, whether God foreknows or foreordains our destinies, whether a thousand angels can dance on the head of a pin. Others sought to control it by finding one authority who could speak plainly and simply for the Fire, an authority like a pope, a tradition, scripture, reason, or emotion. Christians almost dispersed the Fire by going their separate ways, each according to the authority of their choosing.

Two thousand years after the descent and spread of the Pentecost flames, we Christians, for love and fear of God, still seek to institutionalize that Fire in structures of theology and authority. As ridiculous and futile as that may sound, we cannot be blamed for trying. We cannot be blamed for our efforts to control the Fire because it is the nature of the human beast to fear fire. We try to control the Fire without dousing it. But to control a fire, you have to kill it, and this Fire will not die.

Back in the forest, it is night again. The firefighters are gone and the fire has subsided. Smoky haze fills the air with the smell of charred wood. A rabbit ventures timidly into the skeleton brush. Two birds fly overhead. A gentle breeze blows. Suddenly there is a gust. A spark floats up from a hidden ember, sails in the wind over a ditch, and lights on a dry, leafy branch.

CHAPTER 10

A Still, Small Voice

And there he came to a cave, and lodged there; and behold, the word of the LORD came to him, and he said to him, "What are you doing here, Elijah?" He said, "I have been very jealous for the LORD, the God of hosts; for the people of Israel have forsaken thy covenant, thrown down thy altars, and slain thy prophets with the sword; and I, even I only, am left; and they seek my life, to take it away."

And he said, "Go forth, and stand upon the mount before the LORD." And behold, the LORD passed by, and a great and strong wind rent the mountains, and broke in pieces the rocks before the LORD, but the LORD was not in the wind; and after the wind an earthquake, but the LORD was not in the earthquake; and after the earthquake a fire, but the LORD was not in the fire; and after the fire a still small voice. And when Elijah heard it, he wrapped his face in his mantle and went out and stood at the entrance of the cave. And behold, there came a voice to him, and said, "What are you doing here, Elijah?"

1 Kings 19:9–13, RSV

A long drought parched Israel during King Ahab's rule. Dust rose from silent brook beds. Crops wilted or cowered in the depleted soil. Scores of cattle collapsed daily, leaving chalky bones in fields of yellow grass.

Atop Mount Carmel at night, the prophet Elijah sat alone. He could almost hear the thunder and rain in the dreams of the sleeping people below, but the dry breeze blew through skeleton trees, stirring watchful and distant stars. Elijah made himself a fugitive the day he announced the coming of this drought right under Ahab's well-trimmed chin, a drought by which Yahweh judged Ahab's choice of a new god for Israel—Baal, a god of fertility. But on that night Elijah knew that God would render judgment with rain, and just as God called Elijah to announce the drought, God called him to set the stage for the most spectacular epiphany since the parting of the Red Sea.

As day broke and dreams of rain dissipated beneath a cloudless sky, Elijah stepped out of hiding and challenged all four hundred fifty prophets of Baal to a showdown: One hunted, wandering prophet from the desert versus four hundred fifty sophisticated prophets from Canaan's great civilization and culture. One God of liberation, judgment, and passionate mercy versus a domesticated god whose favor priests and kings purchased for a price. One God, unseen and unbridled and unpredictable like the wind, versus a god dug into the soil, a predictable god of consummation and birth and decay. A jealous God with one prophet versus a reasonable god with four hundred fifty prophets.

Standing alone before Ahab, the prophets of Baal, and all the people of Israel, Elijah challenged the establishment prophets to throw away their matches and prepare a bull for sacrifice. They needed only to persuade Baal to light a fire on the dry wood of their altar. "Fair enough" said the prophets of Baal. "The faith of four hundred fifty of us can't lose when pitted against the faith of one fanatical holdout for the outdated God of wilderness days."

With the morning still new, they prepared the bull and smugly called out to Baal to finish this lopsided contest quickly. The sun rose higher and hotter, and they felt their stomachs knotting. They danced around the altar to entertain Baal, lighten him up, wake him up—something. Noon passed as Elijah jeered, reclining under a shady tree. Four hundred fifty prophets of Baal huddled, drenched with sweat, bordering on delirium. They pulled out all the stops, lashing themselves with swords until their blood flowed with their sweat, hoping Baal would catch the most obvious hint.

The sky was as clear and still as death. The dead bull's stench filled the dry air. There was no fire. "There was no voice, no answer, and no response" (1 Kings 18:29). The prophets of Baal stared blankly, their empty spirits sank and crumpled at their feet.

The crowd murmured as Elijah stepped into the light of day and bid them watch. He piled twelve stones to make an altar, chopped wood which he lined up on the altar, then prepared a bull for sacrifice. Upping the ante, he dug a trench around the altar and summoned volunteers from the audience to pour buckets of water on it, saturating wood and bull, filling the trench to overflowing, making holy muck. Then Elijah stepped up to the crowd until they could see the sweat on his face, the dirt in his finger-nails, and the quivering of his lower lip. He lifted his eyes to the cloudless heavens and prayed aloud for God to show these double-minded people that there is only one God, not two, the "God of Abraham, Isaac, and Israel" (1 Kings 18:36), the God who sent Elijah his prophet, the God of their very hearts.

From the clear blue sky something descended that could not be lightning but was lightning, a bolt from beyond the bluest beyond, a fire as white as starlight that, at one and the same time, fraternized with galaxies and torched Elijah's sacrificial bull. It reported like worlds colliding, stopping every heart, paralyzing every leg, dilating every pupil in abject terror. All things went pale for miles around like shadows ambushed by beacons. Yet, in an instant, the only beacon was Elijah's altar where the fire from heaven "licked up the water that was in the trench" (1 Kings 18:38) and not only made embers of the bull but made torches of the stones and dust. As powerfully as that bolt struck, not one splinter scattered, no dust puffed up. Only clouds of crackling smoke streamed to God's heaven.

Adrenalin coursed through Elijah's veins. He smelled

rain in the rising wind, and he could almost hear rain
pound down Israel's dust as it had in the people's dreams
the night before. He commanded those dreaming Israelites to put the four hundred fifty prophets of Baal out of
their misery, and he cavalierly teased King Ahab, prod-
ding him to celebrate the rains that Yahweh, not Baal,
was sending. In a victorious frenzy, almost tasting the
rain, he scaled Mount Carmel again.

Then Elijah's spirit stilled, his heart quieted, and he
bowed low in the pinnacle's shadow, praying, listening as
he had the night before when God attuned his ears to the
people's dreams of rain. In the silence, he heard the beating of his heart and the sound of a companion's feet pick-
ing their way back down and up the peak seven times.
Like the silence, the blue sky spread without limits from
that mountaintop. Finally a cloud approached, a cloud
that came after lightning, not before; a cloud like a lone
hand of greeting, comfort, and power; a small cloud, but a
cloud that signified great things in a land where no one
remembered clouds or great things except in dreams.

Elijah ran like a cyclone down the mountain. He dared
Ahab to get his chariots back to his mansion in Jezreel
before the approaching rains stuck them in the mud. The
wind whipped and shadows descended from black clouds
lathering the whole sky and heaping to heaven. The temperature dropped and walls of rain pounded the dust into
clay as the people danced in the streets, catching gulps of
rain on their wagging tongues. Elijah euphorically ran
seventeen miles through pouring rain, leading Ahab's
chariots into Jezreel.

Elijah's elation soon plummeted to depression as he
learned that God's revelation in lightning, rain, and power
shattered one cumbersome idol Baal, but left untouched
the most elusive and dangerous of the idols: the self.
Ahab's queen, Jezebel, embodied the worship of the self,
the almighty ego with a raw passion so powerful that
Baal and all his prophets cowered at her feet long before
Yahweh hung them all out to dry. Baal and the fertility

cult were the opiate of the people that Jezebel loved to
traffic. She cared not one whit how Elijah whipped Baal.
She would add Elijah's carcass to the stinking common
grave of the Baal prophets for getting the people to worship a royalty and follow a will that was not her own,
that her husband, Ahab, could not manage for her while
she preened herself and ate grapes. She sent Elijah word
in no uncertain terms that he was a dead man.

Elijah believed it. As far as he was concerned, that miracle at the foot of Mount Carmel compared to the parting
of the Red Sea among God's greatest revelations in
power—pure, thundering power. It stopped the people's
hearts, turned those hearts to the one, true God, and made
all cracked, aching feet dance in the rain. If that miracle,
that epiphany, did not overwhelm Ahab and all the powers that be in the region, if Jezebel did not fall to her knees
and repent like a woman in a burning house, then nothing but nothing would usher in the eternal reign of God.

So into the wilderness Elijah retreated, his eyes fixed on
the ground a few feet in front of him, his steps plodding
and heavy. He did not run for his life so much as he
searched for a place to die or at least sleep the rest of his
life away. Somewhere not so far from the middle of nowhere, he sat beneath a broom tree and prayed, "It is
enough; now, O LORD, take away my life, for I am no
better than my ancestors" (1 Kings 19:4). It is as if he
prayed, "Take my life because, just yesterday, my prophecy appeared to end all need for prophecy. My prophecy
seemed to usher in your glory so powerfully that Israel
would forget all other gods, and all kings and queens,
even Ahab and Jezebel, would worship you day and
night. Kill me, put me out of my misery with all the
prophets slain before me because today is just another
day, and Jezebel still lords her despotic whims over us like
a cat toying with a mouse. In every age there have been
Jezebels and Elijahs: Put this Elijah to rest and send another to cope with this Jezebel and the countless Jezebels
to come."

Elijah slept there the sleep of a man who only wanted to avoid waking, but the angel of the Lord fed him and prodded him and fed him again until a flicker of life returned to his eyes and he walked again. He walked in a trance forty days and forty nights until he reached Mount Horeb, the place where God encountered Moses with brilliance that burned Moses' face. At Horeb, God revealed the divine will to Moses after revealing divine power at the Red Sea. So Elijah came there searching for a revelation of wisdom where power had fallen short, a revelation of God that would burn in his memory and sustain him when he returned to the perpetual disappointment that was Israel.

When he arrived at Mount Horeb, he huddled in the darkest corner of a cave because he halfway feared that God would grant his wish and kill him, and he halfway feared that God would not. Then God called out to Elijah, asking him why he hid there, and Elijah answered that the rebellious people and the likes of Jezebel made dead meat of every prophet before him, and apparently he was next. God summoned him to step into the light of day atop Mount Horeb and face the final revelation, the revelation that would make trivia of that lightning-at-the-altar act that burned Baal to the ground. But Elijah froze, waiting for the revelation in that dark corner of the holy mountain.

Then Elijah heard the wind, the wind that started out like a sea breeze and rapidly built into a blast that could drive entire nations into the ocean many miles away. Elijah heard massive trees lose their grip of the earth, their roots slipping and tearing until the trees ripped free and hurtled through the atmosphere. Rocks and boulders caromed from mountain to mountain, and at the height of the blast, rock formations split into pieces with a deafening explosion. While the wind was like God in its raw, invisible force, it was not God. God was not in the wind. The air stilled.

Elijah heard a faint rumbling sound far in the distance, but almost at once it grew closer and louder like a thousand lions as the earth trembled and rocks flew in his cave and the cave became a chaotic, dark blur. The planet seemed to collapse, and a deep sickness penetrated Elijah's core. The earth seemed like a cauldron bursting, and its crust screamed like a demon railing against light and love. It seemed that the cave would collapse, answering Elijah's prayer for death. And while the earthquake mimicked God's seething, inner wrath that would shake the foundations of all creation, the earthquake was not God. God was not in the earthquake. The earth settled, solid and still.

Then a warm gust of air puffed into the cave, followed by a crackling sound that grew louder and louder until it roared. Elijah peeked over a rock to the cave's entrance and saw great flames dancing and rising, and all the valley looked like the surface of the sun. The scorching, suffocating heat seemed certain to bake Elijah alive. While the fire imitated the wild fury of God's spirit, the fire was not God. God was not in the fire. All at once, when Elijah's death seemed sure, the earth cooled in a gentle rain shower, and the smoke lifted.

Elijah waited, his eyes fixed to the mouth of the cave, his ears attuned, as he watched and listened for the spectacle of God's coming. He watched, he listened for something more terrible than wind, earthquake, or fire. The moments passed in perfect stillness, total silence. Elijah heard the beating of his heart, and as more minutes passed, he could hear himself breathing faster and shorter breaths. The minutes seemed like hours as his heart beat louder and faster, echoing in the cave, shaking his ribs until all at once it occurred to him: This stillness, this terrible silence surpassed wind, earthquake, and fire in its awfulness. Once again, all he saw was still, all he heard, silent; for God was in the eerie, still silence of Mount Horeb.

Then Elijah heard something, or thought he heard something: Something as still as the mountain but as small as a droplet of mist or particle of smoke. Something so small that it may have been nothing at all but a passing fancy of a mind grown weary with silence. Something like a voice but too small or too unreal to be a voice. Perhaps it was not a voice, only the longing for a voice by one growing mad with loneliness. Elijah opened his eyes wide and listened intensely to the terrible silence of God.

And he heard it again: Like a lost kitten purring just within earshot. Like a newborn infant whispering to an angel before losing the gift of conversing with angels. Like a mother consoling her child amid a roaring crowd.

Like a Spirit spending eternity wandering the wilderness. It was the voice of a wandering, lonely God who chose a people and set them free and sought communion with them only to see them choose a king and build a walled city while their Lord wandered alone in the wilderness. God spoke in a still, small voice after speaking in thunder centuries before at the Red Sea and days before at the foot of Mount Carmel. Yet, those who heard the thunder soon forgot, and those, like Jezebel, who wanted God to stay in the wilderness and let well enough alone heard nothing at all. So, Elijah heard for the first time the still, small voice with which God would speak until the end of time in unlikely places like Israel, in unlikely people like a carpenter's son, in unlikely followers like a church composed of outright sinners.

Nobody knows what God said to Elijah in that still, small voice. I suppose Elijah found the words too wonderful or too terrible for us to bear. But when he heard the tiny whisper in the wilderness, he knew it was God, the same God revealed just days before in thunder and blackness and rain, in the humiliation of the Canaanite god Baal, and the slaughter of Baal's prophets, every one. Elijah stepped to the mouth of the cave with his face wrapped in his mantle to shield himself from the brilliance of the Lord, the face of God whom no one could see and live to tell about it. God ordered Elijah to appoint the leaders and the prophet through whom God would overthrow the present order of Ahab, Jezebel, and their god Baal.

Elijah took his orders from the same God of thunder who prevailed over Baal days before, the same wild God of the wilderness who set Israel free. But in another sense, this was not the same God, and Elijah was not the same man. Neither of them would be the same again.

CHAPTER 11

The Scandal of Praise

Happy are those
    who do not follow the advice of the wicked,
or take the path that sinners tread,
    or sit in the seat of scoffers;
but their delight is in the law of the Lord,
    and on his law they meditate day and night.
Psalm 1:1–2

Praise the Lord!
Praise God in his sanctuary;
    praise him in his mighty firmament!
Praise him for his mighty deeds;
    praise him according to his surpassing greatness!

Praise him with trumpet sound;
    praise him with lute and harp!
Praise him with tambourine and dance;
    praise him with strings and pipe!
Praise him with clanging cymbals;
    praise him with loud clashing cymbals!
Let everything that breathes praise the Lord!
Praise the Lord!

Psalm 150

The Psalter opens with a blessing and closes with praise, thus demonstrating that the Psalms are scandalous from beginning to end. The Psalms make no bones about the fact that this life is hardly a blessed state. Just a cursory leafing through the Psalter presents enough depression, despair, helplessness, paranoia, and guilt to leave any reasonable person wondering how God can bear to give humankind the time of day. In fact, the very question, "My God, my God, why have you forsaken me?"—later repeated by Jesus on the cross—appears first in a psalm (Ps. 22:1). In the face of all this misery and impotence, the Psalter's opening blessing outright defies common sense before the music even starts.

The music starts nonetheless. King David sings a cappella in Psalm 3, with strings in Psalm 4, with flutes in Psalm 5, and the band plays on. How can this broken one—David or you or me—sing so melodiously, be so blessed? Because of the final scandal: praising the Lord.

Praising God is dangerous business, especially when you consider that God hears the praise. In a condemnation of King Saul, the Lord says to Samuel, "The LORD does not see as mortals see; they look on the outward appearance, but the LORD looks on the heart" (1 Sam. 16:7). In other words, saying "Praise the Lord" and giving a donation may get one into the PTL Club, but God listens to the heart. Praising God scandalizes us because it makes for either the most sublime music in heaven or the cheapest, scheming bluff in the smoke-filled rooms of hell with no middle ground, and mere mortals cannot discern for sure which it is. Only God knows our hearts once and for all.

But we mortals hear praises to God enough to have our opinions. All too often, praises to God have a ring of sentimental self-congratulation. One could as easily sing out, "Everything's Going My Way" or "If My Friends Could See Me Now!" In such a case, praising God is just another form of self-congratulation while acknowledging that God is the benefactor. In other words, the sugar daddy god rewards everyone who says the right words and pulls the right strings.

An essential problem here is that all too often a false god gets the praise while God does not even get a ticket to the concert. The sugar daddy god is not the only impostor who steals the praise. If I believe that God is a white, highly educated, middle-class male like me, my saying, "Praise the

Lord" could ultimately mean, "Praise me." If I believe that God is a Democrat or a Carolina basketball fan or an animal rights activist, my praises for God may boil down to little more than promotion of my narrow cause.

The scandal of praising God—of *truly* praising God—is that I must say it with all my heart, while at the same time I must not know quite what I am saying. If God will not conform to my selfish desires, pet causes, or socioeconomic values, then I cannot very well understand whom I praise. If I anticipate the fulfillment of a glorious kingdom of God unlike any earthly kingdom known to humankind, I cannot very well know what I praise the Lord for. If I cannot identify once and for all the God whom I praise or the promise of the kingdom, how can I praise the Lord?

One answer is that I can praise the Lord as a startled response, with eyes wide open and pupils dilated, because something completely unexpected and wonderful has come into sight. My response may resemble the astonishment of Bob Cratchit on hearing a reformed Ebenezer Scrooge pledge to raise his salary the morning after Christmas. My response may resemble that of a woman cured of blindness who sees the face of her beloved for the first time. Or my response may be breathless and confused and wild-eyed like a shepherd boy who has been running through the fields and the bushes and brambles in pursuit of an angel's promise of a newborn king. If I cannot know God's agenda or comprehend the promise of the kingdom in full, I can open my eyes to partial glimpses of divine glory at unexpected times and places, and I can then praise the name of the Lord.

Or I can praise God, not only in the unexpected moment of epiphany, but in the beating of my heart, the aching of my loneliness, the coldness of the air I breathe, the anticipation of the kingdom's coming. Such praise is almost silent yet almost an explosion, like the echo of a whisper in a deep, dark cave. Such praise acknowledges that "Praise the Lord" is more than just a sentence: It is an action. The saying is the doing and the doing, the saying.

In the long darkness between epiphanies of light, the life absorbed in kindness to fellow sufferers, sustained in prayer that discloses all hope and despair, and quickened with praise that defies the night, becomes a life of melodious praise. In such a life, flesh and blood become praise itself, and praise becomes epiphany.

As Christ reveals himself in unexpected times and places, evidence of such lives of praise can be found in unexpected times and places. For example, one autumn afternoon in Charlotte, North Carolina, my wife and I browsed from booth to booth at a crafts festival. At one booth we read calligraphy prints and found this verse of praise:

> I believe in the sun
> > even when it is not
> > > shining.
> I believe in love
> > even when not
> > > feeling it.
> I believe in God
> > even when He
> > > is silent.

Impressed, I asked the calligrapher for the source. "Nobody knows," he answered. "It was found scrawled on a wall in a Nazi concentration camp." An anonymous life of praise had passed through that place of death.

There are other ways of praising God, I am sure, but only when the heart is truly engaged and the eyes are truly open do we get beyond the predicament of praising an unseen and incomprehensible God. Only then can we proclaim blessings upon those who praise God in the singing of the psalms, in visiting a newborn king in a fly-infested manger, in scrawling a simple poem of faith on the wall of a death camp. Only then does praise transcend our broken, confused motives and become a brave and delightful scandal.

CHAPTER 12

The Great Practical Joke

At that same hour Jesus rejoiced in the Holy Spirit and said, "I thank you, Father, Lord of heaven and earth, because you have hidden these things from the wise and the intelligent and have revealed them to infants; yes, Father, for such was your gracious will. All things have been handed over to me by my Father; and no one knows who the Son is except the Father, or who the Father is except the Son and anyone to whom the Son chooses to reveal him."

Then turning to the disciples, Jesus said to them privately, "Blessed are the eyes that see what you see! For I tell you that many prophets and kings desired to see what you see, but did not see it, and to hear what you hear, but did not hear it."

Luke 10:21–24

In Luke 10:1–24, we read about the Great Practical Joke. Jesus played this grand prank on "the wise and intelligent" of this world and everyone who bets on them, including Satan himself. This elaborate trick humbled the movers and shakers to this day, and it made "Satan fall from heaven like a flash of lightning" (v. 18). Jesus laughed out a prayer into the heavens, splitting a gut in mischievous gratitude to God, rolling on the ground until his disciples propped him up and received his delirious beatitude, "Blessed are the eyes that see what you see!" (v. 23).

The joke went like this: Jesus selected seventy new disciples to go out and change the world. That's right, change the world: Give hope to the hopeless and shame to the shameless. Help the dying look forward to life and the living look forward to death. Make the first last and the last first. Send good news beyond anyone's wildest dreams, and make it so just by sending it. Change the world.

Another messiah might have applied for a grant or started a foundation to pay the best and the brightest to take on this formidable task. The industrious messiah might have arranged interviews at Harvard, Yale, or Stanford to recruit the cream of the graduating class. The more aggressive messiah might pound the Wall Street pavement to coax in some bullish execs with business savvy who show an interest in the spiritual markets. The messiah with clout would pay top dollar for any presidential campaign wizard he could grab to persuade a fickle public mind, and adding a few Nobel laureates to the team for credibility would not hurt a bit either. This team would have the right stuff.

Any other messiah would recruit a dream team, but not the smirking Messiah from Galilee with a trick up his sleeve, not the one and only Jesus Christ. He picked losers on one hand and those with nothing to lose on the other. If a discipleship candidate felt at all torn between the mission and anything worth going home to—a waterbed, a field to plow, a loving family, even a funeral to take care of—no hire. Jesus only wanted those foolish or desperate enough to hand their lives over to a rambling stranger from Galilee who pumped them full of promises of a kingdom but who lacked any rings on his fingers to show for it.

When Jesus gathered them for a pep talk and final instructions, he surveyed some unlikely characters: washed-up madams, regulars on the unemployment line, skid-row bums, Maytag repairmen, ex-cons, ambulance chasers, and Flat Earth Society members. Knowing that Satan loved to eavesdrop at times like this, Jesus said a few lines to give Old Scratch some laughs and set him up for a fall. In solemn tones before his troops, Jesus began, "The harvest is plentiful, but the laborers are few; therefore ask the Lord of the harvest to send out laborers into his harvest" (Luke 10:2).

Satan found it funny enough that Jesus alluded to a "plentiful harvest" of takers for his invisible "kingdom" when humans amount to little more than vain and jealous builders of their own perishable kingdoms. But his muffled laughter burst into a squeal of glee as he heard Jesus refer to this motley crew as his "laborers" for the harvest. Figuring that Jesus must be trying to bait him into action, Satan decided to just sit back and watch Jesus flop.

"See, I am sending you out like lambs into the midst of wolves" (Luke 10:3), Jesus told his ragamuffin troops, and though he kept smiling, Satan stopped laughing because he could see that Jesus knew what he was up against. Then Jesus stacked the odds even further. He told them to go on their mission with no money, no luggage, no charge cards, not even a spare tire, and don't ask directions at any filling stations. For that matter, don't ask for anything, not even a dime for a cup of coffee. Don't talk with anyone on the road. Just trust me. You will get to your destination safe and warm and dry.

He matter-of-factly told them what to expect: Miracles. Approach a house, any house—not every house, just any house—and greet its inhabitants with a word of peace. Whether the place is The Little House on the Prairie or a Mafia hideout, if they respond with a word of peace, there will be peace. You will find peace and hospitality even among wolves because when strangers share words of peace, a third stranger, the Prince of Peace, is not far away.

They will feed you. None of that, "Aw shucks, don't go to any trouble," or, "I'd love to but I'm on duty" claptrap. They may not realize it, you may not have figured it out yet, but the meal is on me. Eat.

Oh, by the way, work a miracle before you leave. Never cleansed a leper or given sight to the blind before? Just do it. You can do it because you're not alone. Don't

waste your time with dreams of opening a medical practice there, and don't say, "Aw, it was the least I could do
in return for the delicious meat loaf and lemon pie."
Peace, healing, wholeness are all about the kingdom. *You*
are all about the kingdom. That is why I am sending you.
Just say, "The kingdom of God has come near to you"
(Luke 10:9), and that will be explanation and blessing
enough for you and your hosts.

In fact, when you come upon a household that does not
welcome you, does not respond with peace when you offer your peace, don't let your nose get bent out of joint.
Don't expect a meal, and don't work any miracles. But say
the same thing, "The kingdom of God has come near to
you." They may laugh at you or chase you out of town,
but they will get the point.

"The kingdom of God has come near." With those
words, you are a doctor to those who love you. With those
same words, you are a judge to those who reject you. For
those who need a judge, dust off your feet and go to the
next place. I will take care of the sentence.

With a charge to go in faith, to offer peace and health,
to bear witness to the kingdom of One who loves and
judges, the seventy disciples left. A bag lady left behind
her bags. A recently fired, alcoholic bus driver left behind
his map. The law student who couldn't pass the bar exam
left behind his excuses. Off they trudged, heads up, sure
of their destinations, two by two.

As they diverged down various dusty roads, Satan
watched from his heavenly corner, grinning smugly,
chalking the tip of a cue stick for a long moment before
turning away to a private game of pool. Jesus sat on a
rock and glanced up with a grin at Satan, who didn't see
Jesus, didn't look his way. The cue ball broke up the fifteen balls with a *crack* that echoed in the clouds like thunder. No balls pocketed.

As Satan played pool, the world—his world—changed.
The Galilean's ship of fools floated. His team of red shirts
and walk-ons won the title. The hopeless gained hope, the

shameless, shame. The dying found new life, and the living found something to die for. The first became last and the last, first. The blind received sight, the lame walked, the lepers were cleansed, the deaf could hear. The dead were raised. Good news came at last to the poor, the have-nots, the losers and those with nothing to lose, and it was delivered by their own kind.

Jesus greeted his euphoric troops as they returned. "Lord, in your name even the demons submit to us!" (Luke 10:17). He joined in the jubilation, proclaiming that "I watched Satan fall from heaven like a flash of lightning," and indeed, the satanic pool table had fallen silent. Jesus pumped them up with their power to overcome evil, and though he took a sober pause to counsel modesty in their claims, he was more intoxicated with the victory than anyone there.

Then he laughed until the tears soaked his cheeks, until his feet would no longer support him, until he could no longer sit but rolled in the dusty road, the most motley fool of them all. Almost exhausted, he flopped onto his back and deliriously addressed the heavens in prayer. "I thank you, Father, Lord of heaven and earth, because you have hidden these things from the wise and the intelligent and have revealed them to infants," he prayed and then convulsed with giggling over the irony of it all.

"Yes, Father, for such was your gracious will," he added in a breathless doxology. Then a calm satisfaction laid him still there on that road on his back, and he concluded, "All things have been handed over to me by my Father; and no one knows who the Son is except the Father, or who the Father is except the Son and anyone to whom the Son chooses to reveal him."

That, of course, was the joke, that no one really knows the Father who made all things or the Son through whom all things were made. No one except this motley crew of chosen ones, these losers with nothing left to lose. The wise and intelligent look for answers in their textbooks. The movers and shakers look for answers in their pocket-books. But the ones who leave their textbooks and pocket-books behind to heed the Son's outlandish answers rejoice in the end, for their names are written in heaven. They are blessed, for they see and hear what prophets and kings desired to see and hear but never did: The face of the Son. The sound of the Word. The laughter of God.

As for Satan, he did not play his last game of pool that day. He did not even get in his last laugh, for the wise and intelligent still serve him with their plans and schemes for human kingdoms. The movers and shakers still invest their capital in personal towers of Babel. But Satan fell like lightning from the heavens that day when he thought he had a day off. He has not had a day off since. And it was not his last fall.

PART II

Ironies of Life and Death

Listen, I will tell you a mystery! We will not all die, but we will all be changed, in a moment, in the twinkling of an eye, at the last trumpet. . . . Then the saying that is written will be fulfilled:

"Death has been swallowed up in victory."

"Where, O death, is your victory?

Where, O death, is your sting?"

1 Corinthians 15:51–52a, 54b–55

CHAPTER 13

The Heart's Desire

Moses said, "Show me your glory, I pray." And [the LORD] said, "I will make all my goodness pass before you, and will proclaim before you the name, 'The LORD'; and I will be gracious to whom I will be gracious, and will show mercy on whom I will show mercy. But," he said, "you cannot see my face; for no one shall see me and live."

Exodus 33:18–20

Thomas said to him, "Lord, we do not know where you are going. How can we know the way?" Jesus said to him, "I am the way, and the truth, and the life. No one comes to the Father except through me. If you know me, you will know my Father also. From now on you do know him and have seen him."

Philip said to him, "Lord, show us the Father, and we will be satisfied." Jesus said to him, "Have I been with you all this time, Philip, and you still do not know me? Whoever has seen me has seen the Father."

John 14:5–9

I long for love, but I fear it. I long for peace, but I cannot let things be. I long for truth, but I lie to myself every day. I long for faith, but I cannot loosen my grip on every little thing that concerns me.

I kick against the goads. "I do not do the good I want, but the evil I do not want is what I do" (Rom. 7:19), says Paul, speaking a truth that I want to confess but cannot bear to utter. My passions are my privations, my bliss is my loss, my yearnings are my terrors.

I am no stranger. You know me well. You would know me better if I did not frighten you so with my contradictions. I look back at you in the mirror. I am Adam. I am you.

My longings and fears are one. What do I long for most? What is my heart's desire? To see the face of God, the face that would strike me dead with abject terror if I caught but a glimpse of it.

I "heard the sound of the Lord God walking in the garden at the time of the evening breeze" (Gen. 3:8). The evening breeze in Eden. Until that evening, that cool breeze was honey and my nakedness a palate. Only the woman beside me could quicken my flesh more.

That evening the breeze made us shiver. The nakedness that made us free and intimate became a shell of shame. We sought to become like gods, though the one God warned us not to. Be careful what you ask for, you might get it. We became like gods—creature-gods: Creatures disquieted with dreams of being more than creatures. Gods burdened with nightmares of being less than gods.

We were ashamed of our nakedness because we had such contradictory feelings about it. We longed for the comforting face of God, but the thought of that face emptied our spirits, filled us with dread. We heard the sound of the Lord God walking with steps like those of an executioner in a long hallway. It was the time of the chilling evening breeze.

Thousands of years pass. For God these thousands of years are but the falling of a raindrop into a lake. For us, these thousands of years are thousands of promises made and broken, thousands of births, wanted and unwanted, thousands of deaths, noble and senseless.

I am Moses. You follow me because you were a slave, and now you are free. The hidden God sent me to lead you to the place your mothers and fathers died for, the place your daughters and sons live for. You do not know why I was chosen. You only know that we were chosen together. I do not know why God chose me. I feel bewildered every time the Lord calls. Because God set you free, you send me to give voice to your gratitude. Because God set you free, you send me to give voice to your indignation.

Let us share a secret. You and I share something else in common. We long to see the face of God. Yes, I know that when the Holy One came to the top of Mount Sinai in fire and clouds, you scurried into your tents like frightened moles. Do you think that I was more than a frightened mole when I stood in God's presence? The divine face is a mystery, yes, a mystery too great for us to speak of. But the greatest mystery of which we can speak is the mystery of our hearts, the mystery that we fear God's face but long for it so. Let me tell you how I know.

You broke the covenant, the promise that God chooses you and you live in grateful obedience. You built a god of bronze with a face you could see. Of course I was angry. I saw the false god's face and smashed the tablets with God's commandments because you were not worthy of them. But in the pathetic statue, I saw your longing to see the divine face. God summoned me to a meeting.

When I went, I took your longing with me as you cowered in fear. I thought God might crush me as an example to you. But God was merciful. We conversed intimately. Our Lord said to me, "I know you by name, and you have also found favor in my sight" (Ex. 33:12), all the while knowing my heart, knowing that I wanted to see the face of my maker, and loving me anyway. I said that I needed a companion, that we needed a companion, someone to protect us in hostile territory. God knew my heart and became our companion, our protector, just as I wished without my saying it. "My presence will go with you, and I will give you rest" (v. 14), our Lord assured me.

The face of God would go with me. I was riddled with dread and desire at once. I tried to say it. I tried to speak my heart's desire and terror, your heart's desire and terror. But I stopped a hair short: "Show me your glory, I pray." Surely, I thought, the Lord knows my longing. For that insane moment, I would have died to see God's face.

With a voice that was more than loving, a voice that was love, the Lord God answered, "I will make all my goodness pass before you, and will proclaim before you the name, 'Yahweh,' and I will be gracious to whom I will be gracious, and will show mercy on whom I will show mercy. But you cannot see my face; for no one shall see me and live." So God passed before me and blocked my view with a great hand. Then I saw the Lord's back, the back that shouldered the thousands of our years of grace and brutality, living and dying, longing and fearing. The back that shouldered us when we could not carry on.

I did not know the face of God. But I knew my heart's desire. I knew your heart's desire. The Lord parted in a gentle breeze that blew the clouds away.

Thousands of years pass. You, Philip, and I, Thomas, are disciples of one who is, in a sense, gone but who is, in a greater sense, still present. He was a teacher who was more than a teacher, a healer who was more than a healer, a man named Jesus who was more than a man. We did not know who he was, but he bid us follow, and we did. Never had we seen so much in a face.

He bid us farewell one day. Jesus seemed to know he was about to die, and he spoke of his death as if it were more than death, as if it were somehow our only hope. He spoke in words that were more than words. He spoke in contradictions to disciples who listened with contradictory hearts. His death was hope, somehow. The death of our leader would show us the way to our heart's desire: the face of God.

As you and I sat near him, our eyes met. We confided in each other once that we both found it baffling, our following this strange teacher. After long hours we agreed that somehow we knew that this man held the secret to our heart's desire if anyone did. Also we agreed that, like Moses, we longed to see the face of God and live.

Like Moses conversing intimately with the Lord on Mount Sinai, I asked Jesus indirectly if he would accompany us forever on our journey to find our heart's desire. "Lord, we do not know where you are going. How can we know the way?" I asked.

His answer was too good, too terrible: "I am the way, and the truth, and the life. No one comes to the Father except through me. If you know me, you will know my Father also. From now on you do know him and have seen him." I know him? I have seen him? "No one shall see me and live," said God to Moses. Were Jesus' words assurance of my heart's desire or a curse of death? I blinked rapidly.

You cut to the quick, "Lord, show us the Father, and we will be satisfied." You looked intently at him with the same blissful, suicidal madness that must have appeared on the face of Moses as he appealed for a glimpse at the face of God. Surely Jesus would answer with double-talk, with some half measure, with, at best, some glimpse at God's mighty shoulders but not at the face of God. "Whoever has seen me has seen the Father," he answered. The warm wind blew in your hair. Your face was stone.

Two thousand years later, we gather, a people with a preposterous claim. We have seen the face of God. We died. We live to tell about it.

I am Adam. I hear the Lord walking in the garden at the time of the evening breeze. I hide, naked, ashamed. I am with the woman. I am alone. I glance about frantically for anything but God's face. I look to my feet and see a newborn infant, his face red and puffy, his eyes tightly closed. It is the face of Almighty God, and the contradiction kills me. I am judged by a newborn. I die through the ages for that child. Eve picks him up and rocks him.

I am Moses. I hear our Lord talking to me in intimate tones. I receive the law and hear the command to take it to the people, the children, the lambs of God. In the giving and the commanding, God fulfills the law even before I take a step. Such power is too great for me. With a trembling whisper, I ask to see God's face, and from the shadows, Jesus steps before me. His face is too terrible to see, bruised and bloody, his body whipped and broken. Hungry, naked, persecuted, he blesses me, and in blessing me he judges me. I die, my heart broken.

I am Thomas, his disciple. I have seen his broken body nailed to a cross while I cowered in the shadows. I heard Christ cry out in Godforsakenness. I saw the anguish in his face from the nails and the sword. I saw the blood run down his face from a mocking crown of thorns. I saw his chest heave and the life drain from his cheeks as his eyes rolled upward. I saw them take him down, his face another face of death at the hands of mortals.

Now I hear rumors that he lives again, but I live with my feet on the ground. I know what I saw. My blood still runs cold from the sight of his suffering. I must see and touch not only the face of the man but the wounds before I can believe such tales. Then he appears, his face full of life and peace, offering to let me touch his wounds, but just the seeing and the hearing kills me, kills the old man with his feet on the ground. I exclaim, "My Lord and my God!" (John 20:28). My heart's desire! In a moment, I die. In a moment, I live.

We are church. We listen to God's word. We catch one another's eye because we know our heart's desire. We catch one another's eye, and we see the face of our Lord. We die together. We live in Christ. God's morning breeze makes our flesh tingle with newness.

CHAPTER 14

The Race against Death

Therefore I tell you, do not worry about your life, what
you will eat or what you will drink, or about your body,
what you will wear. Is not life more than food, and the
body more than clothing? Look at the birds of the air; they
neither sow nor reap nor gather into barns, and yet your
heavenly Father feeds them. Are you not of more value
than they? And can any of you by worrying add a single
hour to your span of life?

Matthew 6:25–27

I ramble down the aisles of the grocery store, pushing a
shopping cart that bounces and bangs as if on cobble-
stone. In my left hand, I carry a checklist of products
scientifically derived from the most current data available
on nutrition, health, and mortality. Heart disease is the
leading cause of death in the United States. I select low-
sodium sweet peas, high-fiber cereal without palm oil,
and ground turkey instead of ground beef. Cancer trails
not far behind heart disease as a cause of death, so I by-
pass carcinogenic, saccharin-laced products and sneer at a
stack of cigarette cartons. The next leading cause of death
is traffic accidents, so I keep my cart on the right-hand
side of the aisle and look both ways as I approach a new
aisle, halting just in time to avoid a lethal broadside
smash from an out-of-control, caffeine-fueled shopper
with a cart full of fatback, flour, and Coca-Cola twelve-
packs.

After selecting the last item on my list, I skillfully nego-
tiate my overburdened, limping cart between darting chil-

dren, around two gossiping couples with their carts jamming the canned meats section, and past an elderly woman pushing her cart at a slower, saner pace down the homestretch. On arriving at the checkout area, I survey the lines to find the one with the optimal combination of few carts, few groceries, and efficient personnel. Also, I avoid any line occupied by some smart shopper waving a fistful of time-wasting coupons. Eventually I select a line that, while not the shortest, sports lightly loaded carts, a checkout person who has worked there since the era before computer scanners, and a puny but spunky bag boy with catlike hands. I take my place in line and glance at a tabloid headline: "Farmer Shoots 23-lb. Grasshopper."

In his own way, that farmer won the race I run so frantically at the grocery store. He may eat biscuits, gravy, bacon, and eggs each morning before stuffing a wad of snuff in his cheek, but he made it to the front page of the *Weekly World News* and I did not. His picture stands out on the rack, even beside photos of a TV starlet sporting a scandalous weight gain and the micro-bikini-clad girlfriend of the media's favorite millionaire playboy. With a satisfied grin the farmer holds the insect by its hind legs like a prize catch. This is his moment of immortality.

I, on the other hand, leave no stone unturned in my bid to add a minute or two to my life by subtracting a few grams of saturated fat from my diet and by eliminating idle moments in the checkout line. Never mind that lowering my risk of heart failure, cancer, or shopping-cart accidents does not change the fact that I must die of something someday. Never mind that life is just as precious in a supermarket checkout line as it is in the maddening traffic on the boulevard which greets me after the groceries are bagged and paid for. If I can add a few days to my life, who knows, I may live long enough to shoot a *twenty-four* pound grasshopper and join the ranks of the immortal farmer.

I run a race at home, at work, on vacation, and even at

church. It is the same race I run at the grocery store. It is the race against death.

Flick on the news this evening and watch the report on the local, worldwide, and national race against death. The President's heart weakens for a short time while jogging, and the nation holds its collective breath: What about the race, the résumé? Yes, he has had an impressive political career, but there is much more to be done. Never mind the man who is the same man whether he is chief executive or chief dogcatcher, the little boy masked in heavy White House protocol, the child of God. If he dies, will the Vice President pass muster?

In other news, the aforementioned millionaire playboy gets his time on the TV with a report of his latest financial dabblings. This upscale racer against death broadcasts loud and clear that he has it all, anything your heart may desire or lust after and then some, not to mention a constant place in the limelight. Having it all, he wants more because death sets an unacceptable limit, making even everything he has not quite enough. He only takes the race that all of us run to its logical conclusion. A bumper sticker reads: The One Who Dies with the Most Toys Wins. If that is the object of the game, the media's darling millionaire playboy wins.

But that is not the object of life—real life—and far be it from me to judge whether our wealthy friend wins or loses in life because I run the same futile race he runs, only on a smaller scale. Even if I abhor glitz and greed, thumbing my Calvinistic nose at extravagance, I race against death just like the millionaire playboy and everyone else. I race against death when I shop at the grocery store. I race against death when I scramble for financial security, letting the bottom line guide my decisions. I race against death when I worry over my career, whether I am reaching my potential or missing my calling. I race against death when I puzzle darkly over love, whether I get enough or give enough. I race against death when I worry over being moral, whether I contribute to society or have no worth. In a race against death, a race to get enough health, security, career satisfaction, love, or virtue before it is all over, death can only win.

Jesus blows the whistle on this race, and if we are honest, we have to admit that we do not much like it when he does. "Look at the birds of the air," he bids us as if we have time to watch birds. "They neither sow nor reap nor gather into barns, and yet your heavenly Father feeds them. Are you not of more value than they?" he asks rhetorically. "Well, maybe," we respond. "But God helps those who help themselves, so if you don't mind, I've got to figure out which one of these cereals has the most soluble fiber." Jesus persists, "Can any of you by worrying add a single hour to your span of life?" This question cuts to the quick, exposing our darkest doubts about the race we run, so we try to ignore him.

We do a pretty good job of ignoring him because there is really no place for the likes of Jesus in this race against death. He took no part in it two thousand years ago when he walked this earth, or if he did he certainly did not play by the rules and did not play very well either. At the height of his career, he turned and walked straight into Jerusalem, knowing full well that the authorities there wanted him dead. Then what did he do? He walked into the Temple at high noon with a whip and wrecked the place, driving out all the peddlers and small-time merchants, trashing the bake sale for summer youth missions to Cocoa Beach and leaving the church bazaar, which was approved by the church session, in a shambles. They nailed him up within a week.

So it looks like he lost in the race against death, but in fact, he was not even playing the game. He knew we would not really listen to his lovely parables about the birds of the air or the lilies of the field. We might put them to music, but we would not really get the point that this all-consuming race against death is as futile as trying to grow another foot taller, that in fact, there is another game in town, a costly game, but a game you cannot lose if you abide by one simple rule: Follow him. Too caught up in the complexities of racing against death, we seldom take his simple game and its one rule very seriously. Since we do not listen to his words about birds and lilies, he did his talking with his hands and feet, his flesh and blood. He died for us.

He rose again from the dead, I might add, and in doing so, he made it clear that the joke is on me with my scientifically selected groceries, the millionaire playboy with his new casino and new girl, and the farmer with his twenty-three-pound grasshopper. Jesus made it clear that the race against death is passé, over, kaput, washed up, and there is a new game in town that death cannot win. None of us can be sure what his promise of eternal life fully entails, but one thing is for sure: Even if we die in a shopping cart collision, our lives will be complete, meaningful, and whole in him regardless of how we run the race against death. All we have to do to enjoy the blessing of life is shun the rules of the race and follow him. Our heavenly Father will take it from there.

CHAPTER 15

The Experiment

> After these things God tested Abraham. He said to him,
> "Abraham!" And he said, "Here I am." He said, "Take
> your son, your only son Isaac, whom you love, and go to
> the land of Moriah, and offer him there as a burnt offering
> on one of the mountains that I shall show you." . . .
>
> When they came to the place that God had shown him,
> Abraham built an altar there and laid the wood in order.
> He bound his son Isaac, and laid him on the altar, on top
> of the wood. Then Abraham reached out his hand and
> took the knife to kill his son. But the angel of the Lord
> called to him from heaven, and said, "Abraham, Abra-
> ham!" And he said, "Here I am." He said, "Do not lay
> your hand on the boy or do anything to him; for now I
> know that you fear God, since you have not withheld your
> son, your only son, from me . . .
>
> Because you have done this, . . . I will indeed bless you,
> and I will make your offspring as numerous as the stars of
> heaven and as the sand that is on the seashore. And your
> offspring shall possess the gate of their enemies, and by
> your offspring shall all the nations of the earth gain bless-
> ing for themselves, because you have obeyed my voice."
>
> *Genesis 22:1–2, 9–12, 16–18*

Late one July afternoon, I prop my feet up in my recliner,
take a bite out of a banana, and read the Old Testament.
My two cats curl up in the warm, early evening air lazily
filtering through the window screens. A robin sings overhead, and I hear the playful voices of a man, children, and
a barking dog down the hill next to my apartment. A

locust's cry then drowns out all sounds for a loud, long moment, and as the cry fades, all humans and beasts silently honor the call of the unseen locust. My wife laughs in the bedroom where she talks on the phone with a friend. A cat stretches.

As I reach Genesis, chapter 22, I peel my banana, then I read God's call, "Abraham!" Abraham answered, "Here I am," as confused and hopeful and frightened as anyone would be if summoned out of the blue by God. Then God commanded: "Take your son, your only son Isaac, whom you love, and go to the land of Moriah, and offer him there as a burnt offering on one of the mountains that I shall show you." The cat finishes her leisurely stretch and bathes behind her companion's ears with her pink sandpaper tongue. A four-wheel-drive truck pokes its way down a gravel road nearby. My banana lies forgotten on a lampstand. I taste nothing. My heart is wrenched.

"Surely Abraham protests," I plead quietly, desperately. Surely not. Abraham grimly rose the next morning before the rooster called, readied his beast and servants, and chopped wood for the sacrificial fire, his jaw set, facing his task like a Wyoming farmer staring down the first north winds of winter. He awakened his son, Isaac, telling him to hurry up because they had to take a trip. What do I make of Abraham, who would obey such a command, such a God?

For that matter, what do I make of anyone who would obey an arbitrary command to hurt, even kill, another human being? Thirty years ago, forty men volunteered to participate in a psychological experiment on learning and memory at Yale University. Each subject entered a laboratory full of high-tech equipment, where a cordial experimenter in a gray lab coat greeted him with dispatch and introduced him to a friendly, middle-aged, Irish American fellow. The experimenter designated the Irish man the learner and the subject the teacher. Then he explained that the teacher would test the learner's memory of word pairs and administer electrical shocks for each error. After strapping the learner down in an isolated room and attaching electrodes to his arm, the experimenter escorted the teacher to an adjacent room and sat him down before a panel of switches labeled with voltages ranging from 15 to 450 volts. The experimenter instructed the teacher to read out word pairs to the learner, test his memory of the word pairs on repeated trials, and administer progressively higher shocks for each error. The purpose of this procedure, the experimenter explained, was to study the effects of punishment on learning and memory.

That was a lie, of course. It was a study of obedience, and the designer of the study, Stanley Milgram, wanted to know how much shock the teacher would administer before disobeying the experimenter and calling it quits. Unbeknownst to the teacher, the Irish fellow did not really receive shocks. As the voltage levels increased with each error, the teacher heard him scream, pound the wall, complain frantically of heart problems, and at the highest voltages, respond with dead silence. Milgram predicted that few of the forty subjects would administer the highest levels of shock, but twenty-six of the forty did, and of the remaining subjects, nobody stopped the madness at a voltage below 300.

In obedience to God, Abraham experienced something very much like what Milgram's subjects went through in obedience to an experimenter in a gray lab coat. I can think of no compelling reason why Abraham or I, for that matter, would have responded differently from Milgram's subjects at Yale. This experiment convicts me of the very thing I abhor in Abraham's obedience: willingness to commit a horrible, senseless act simply because somebody told me to do it. If so many of us would torture and perhaps kill an innocent person in obedience to a scientist in a gray lab coat, we would be no less obedient to God Almighty breathing down our necks.

I sit foolishly in my recliner, unsure whether to read on. I pick up the half-eaten banana, rotate it on my fingers as I contemplate it, then put it back down without taking a bite. Running children laugh and scream. My wife hangs up the phone and starts loading clothes in the washer. God doesn't say a word.

This story of Abraham, Isaac, and God is not the story of a psychological experiment. Milgram's subjects administered what they thought were electrical shocks to a kindly gentleman in another room whom they had known for a few minutes. Abraham laid his only son on the altar, tied him down, and reached for a knife.

Just moments before laying his son down, "Isaac said to his father Abraham, 'Father!' And he said, 'Here I am, my son.' He said, 'The fire and the wood are here, but where is the lamb for a burnt offering?' Abraham said, 'God himself will provide the lamb for a burnt offering, my son' " (Gen. 22:7–8). If Abraham ever taught his son a lesson in faith that made the old man sick to teach it, it was then because his son was a boy, a lamb. At the same time, Abraham was reassuring himself, hoping against hope that God had cast off the gray lab coat and gone searching for a real lamb, another lamb to shed its blood to help make things right with God.

It is getting dark outside, and the tree frogs know it, announcing it frantically as if they had never before seen darkness. The laughing children are safely in their homes. The cats practice kung fu, their ears back, their fangs bared, laughing quietly the way fighting cats laugh when they love each other, the way Sarah laughed when she overheard God announce that she would bear a son in old age. The kind of laugh people laugh when they try to hide their laughter from a God they cannot hide from—a stern, watchful God in a gray lab coat. Sarah knew she was caught laughing, so she named her son Isaac, meaning "laughter," right under God's nose, and God took off his gray lab coat and laughed along with her.

Sarah's son, Laughter, the apple of Abraham's eye, the object of all their longing through years of travail and hardship and waiting, lay there on that altar, and if Abraham's obedience in laying him there was merely human, it was also extraordinary. Heartbroken, appalled that the God who had always been so faithful could ask for a sacrifice as senseless and cruel as this, Abraham obeyed. Certainly better than I, Abraham knew that we cannot confine God to our ideas of what God ought to be like even if that means we cannot expect God always to be moral or decent on our terms. So Abraham proceeded with the sordid task because God was God and he, Abraham, was dust.

Indeed God was God, and God demonstrated what it means to be God. "Abraham, Abraham!" the angel of the Lord cried out, and Abraham answered, "Here I am." The angel, almost weeping, spoke for God, "Do not lay your hand on the boy or do anything to him; for now I know that you fear God, since you have not withheld your son, your only son, from me." Abraham saw a ram in a thicket for the sacrifice. Soon Isaac stood there, unstrapped and laughing. From far away, from as nearby as Abraham's own heart, God laughed, and Abraham and Sarah's Laughter lived. Throughout the ordeal, Abraham kept the faith that God would provide a Lamb, a faith that would be his legacy along with an endless line of descendants that began with Laughter.

The cats now run about the apartment, leaping from piano to love seat to table in a mad tear. My wife starts the washer and wonders aloud why the apartment smells like a banana. The monotony of the tree frogs and crickets singing sounds far away. God is terrible. God is gracious. Obedience is common. Obedience is extraordinary. I cannot obey such a God. I cannot help but obey such a God, not only because I am merely human like Milgram's subjects, but because God is God, the God who carries me, the God who surprises me with grace even in mundane moments on dog days like today. The cats stop their playing and poise themselves, their green eyes staring unselfconsciously into mine, and we silently laugh together as cats and humans do when they hear love in the echoes of God's resounding silence and laughter.

CHAPTER 16

The Perfect Rainbow

"I establish my covenant with you, that never again shall all flesh be cut off by the waters of a flood, and never again shall there be a flood to destroy the earth." God said, "This is the sign of the covenant that I make between me and you and every living creature that is with you, for all future generations: I have set my bow in the clouds, and it shall be a sign of the covenant between me and the earth. When I bring clouds over the earth and the bow is seen in the clouds, I will remember my covenant that is between me and you and every living creature of all flesh; and the waters shall never again become a flood to destroy all flesh. When the bow is in the clouds, I will see it and remember the everlasting covenant between God and every living creature of all flesh that is on the earth." God said to Noah, "This is the sign of the covenant that I have established between me and all flesh that is on the earth."

Genesis 9:11–17

First thing every morning, when I am barely conscious enough to know where I am, I grope and stumble through the predawn darkness to my television. I turn it on to listen to the friendly weather lady who just returned from maternity leave. She stands before a U.S. map, and with each movement, each graceful sweep of her hand, she seems to orchestrate the coming and going of rain and sun, cold and heat, wind and calm. Her warm smile and clear, easy speech make her science seem almost friendly.

Surely she has forgotten more about predicting the

weather than I will ever know, and as much as I may complain about her errors, the bottom line is that she is on TV and I am not. She is alert and informed, while I squint in the TV's purple light and would not know the day of the week had she not told me. She looks exquisite in her smart, flowing postmaternity outfit, while my hair looks elephant-chewed, and I wear my bathrobe inside out. She makes her report right on cue without missing a beat, while I feed raisin bran to the cats and pour Meow Mix into my cereal bowl.

Anyone with such grace, poise, and postnatal good humor as the weather lady exhibits for all of Georgia at 6:30 A.M. must live better than I do. Her sensitive, liberated husband who changes the baby's diaper while she tells Atlanta about the jet stream would doubtless agree that she lives quite well. But in spite of her good fortune, I feel a sober sense of common fate with her because we share something in common, something better expressed by my disheveled, half-dressed, stupefied state.

We are both members of the human race, she and I, and as such we both live in peril. Our lives hang in the balance before forces much greater than ourselves, forces such as the weather, for a start. She may make her science seem sweet with her smooth-as-syrup delivery, but her language betrays the threat: High-pressure system in the gulf, low-pressure system in the Tennessee Valley. Gale-force winds, and meanwhile, an Arctic front. Traveler's advisory. Flash-flood watch in effect.

Then she reports on nationwide airport delays, bringing to mind the quiet peril of air travel. When we fly, our lives hang in the balance, suspended 30,000 feet up in a jumbo jet. I recall an idle moment on a flight several years back. Thirty thousand feet above the face of the planet, a lady finished her crossword puzzle, a businessman sorted through his briefcase, a college student was lost in a reverie, and a nervous man in an aisle seat coughed and quaked and perspired as he felt the full 30,000-foot drop in his bone marrow. I gazed out the window at a grand canyon of milky clouds, and I saw something that took my breath away.

A rainbow was suspended just above the cloud cover, but this was not just any rainbow. This rainbow lacked endpoints because there was no horizon to break it into a semicircle, no earth or ocean in sight. So the rainbow made a perfect circle. There, cruising miles above the planet's surface, I saw one rainbow as God must see all rainbows: a perfect array of colors in a perfect circle against the soft, radiant whiteness of the clouds and the gentle, airy blueness of infinite space.

What a lovely sight for God with eyes weary from watching the madness of earth, the Lord's chosen planet in the Milky Way! Before there were weather ladies or jumbo jets or even rainbows, God spied a formless nothing, a churning of chaotic waters with a heart of utter darkness lost in the cosmos. The Lord sent a great wind there and said, "Let there be light for God's sake. Let there be seas and land and vegetation and time. Let there be creatures, and among the creatures let there be man and woman, created in my image." Then with a smile and a touch of sadness, God said, "It is good," very good, but it would not be this good again for a long time.

The creatures made in the Lord's image would come to worship the image and forget the God. They would fancy that they know good and evil as God knows it, and they would try to order and master the world as only God can. In so doing, they would sin and get more and more skilled at sinning. They would build their economies on exploitation rather than justice. Charity would become professionalism, and love would become pornography. The human community would splinter into smaller and smaller in-groups and out-groups until all that would remain would be the lonely, self-interested individual. Cain would kill Abel in a field, Nazi would kill Jew in a gas chamber, American would kill Japanese in a nuclear hell. God, bleary-eyed, would send a flood to drown out all the rascals, sparing only a solid survivor named Noah, who constructed a large sea vessel called an ark and gathered his family and a small zoo in there to ride out the storm to come.

And so it came. When the rains ended, only Noah's ark remained, a drifting speck on the watery orb. The rainbow, the weightless circle of brilliant color, hung above the white cloud cover, unbroken by the horizon of death far below. After forty days of rainfall uninterrupted by human madness, God might have felt tempted to avoid the pain of another human fall. With just one finger, the Lord could dunk the ark, drowning Noah and the whole zoo. God could have hurled the soaked planet like a waterlogged baseball into another galaxy, letting Earth return to its original chaos and churning and darkness. Then God could sit back for the rest of forever and contemplate the beauty of the perfect, circular rainbow without earth's noise disrupting the cosmos, without the planet's violent horizon breaking the rainbow's curve.

When she brought another life into the world several months earlier, the friendly weather lady assumed that God is good, that God says "yes" to life. I assumed the goodness of God when I crawled out of bed to face another weather report and when I took a window seat on the plane. But eons ago, seasick Noah sat exhausted in the dark, smelly ark, numb with grief for his former world washed into oblivion. If he ever assumed, as most of us do, that God is good, that the Creator loves the creation and its creatures, that the Lord says yes to life, his assumption lay below in the deep waters of planet Earth. When the rains ended and God suspiciously eyed the ark drifting on a planet of water, it all hung in the balance.

I suppose God decided that day not to be an indifferent God who creates and says, "It is good," with proper aesthetic distance, but a God who creates and says, "It is good," with love, a love that won't quit. The Lord let the waters subside, ushered frightened, rattled Noah into the light of a new day, and showed him the rainbow, a perfect circle to God, a broken semicircle to Noah, but resplendent with color for both. "You and your descendants will more than likely make jerks of yourselves again," God seemed to say, "but look at this rainbow. Ain't it lovely! When I have just about had it up to here with you and yours, that rainbow will remind me who I am. And that will be your saving grace."

In the millennia to come, there would be more sin and death, more floods and plane crashes, and neither Noah nor the weather lady can explain how God can be good while suffering continues. But the course of human history with all its madness and pain has been punctuated by visions of rainbows, by glimpses of who our Lord is. God bids us look. We see the weather lady's smile, our own distorted reflection in the TV tube, the anguished face of a suffering Christ, a rainbow. In seeing these things, we somehow find something to believe in, even as our lives hang in the balance. We believe in the promise of God's perfect, unbroken rainbow, and that is our saving grace.

CHAPTER 17

A Droplet of Time

A Samaritan woman came to draw water, and Jesus said to her, "Give me a drink." . . . The Samaritan woman said to him, "How is it that you, a Jew, ask a drink of me, a woman of Samaria?" (Jews do not share things in common with Samaritans.) Jesus answered her, "If you knew the gift of God, and who it is that is saying to you, 'Give me a drink,' you would have asked him, and he would have given you living water."

John 4:7, 9–10

You awaken in the middle of the night with yesterday's memories and tomorrow's imaginings going in circles in your mind. Images recur: The face of your boss. A memo full of double-talk. A near accident on the freeway. An argument with your son. All you want is sleep, but the wanting gets in the way, and neither yesterday nor tomorrow will give you any peace tonight. In stuporous, grumbling exasperation, you finally get out of bed and trudge like a zombie to the bathroom. You splash tap water on your hands and face. Before your eyes can adjust to the bathroom light, you turn it off and step into the hall only to find that your vision is no longer adjusted to the darkness.

As you grope toward the kitchen, something almost indiscernible awakens you further, opens your eyes to the deep darkness. Perhaps a strange stirring in your soul alerts you, or the depth of the darkness, or the terrible realization that you have forgotten images of yesterday and cast aside images of tomorrow, leaving you only with the darkness and disorientation and hunger of now. You pause in the dark hallway and reflect, in spite of yourself and with a barely conscious sense of urgency, that this moment culminates every moment you have ever lived and that every moment you have ever lived might as well be this moment of darkness and stillness and restless hunger. Every moment you have ever lived is gone forever, and the only moment you have is this strange one in the lonely night as you stand disheveled and stuporous in your bathrobe. All your memories, all your past with all its kisses and tears and voices and thunderclaps and embarrassments are distilled in your own small brain down to one smaller droplet of recollection in this most insignificant of moments.

Death must be this dark, you imagine, and the moment before death must be like this moment, a droplet of time into which all your past condenses, only to evaporate in another brief time. The most terrible dimension of death must be that last sweet moment of memory when all your years become a dissipating instant. Then darkness.

You walk into the kitchen without turning on the light, and you sit at the table, staring into the darkness, hoping that your eyes will adjust to it and that your now throbbing heart will adjust to the idea of death. Instead your eyelids close, darker still. Your heart slows and your breathing slows and deepens as you try to forget death by thinking of the water splashing on your face moments before. Soon enough, you sleep, and you fall into a dream, a dream that you are a silent, unseen observer two thousand years ago, watching a man at a well, hearing the sounds of water.

Two thousand years ago, Jesus sat by Jacob's well and sent his disciples away for groceries. Jesus sent them away because he wanted time alone to collect his thoughts about where he was coming from and where he was going, about his memories and imaginings. As he sat in the heat, tired from the morning's journey, a woman drew water from the well, and the stirring and pouring sound entranced him. He listened to the melody of water stirring and pouring, stirring and pouring, music to the ears of a thirsty man sitting beneath a high, noonday sun. The sound of the water so entranced him that he forgot where he was coming from and where he was going, and he only thought of where he was then in that insignificant moment.

He was in Samaria, a strange land for a Jew, and he felt a wave of loneliness. Jacob's well marked the burial ground of Joseph, Jacob's son, ground that was the last of many gifts of a doting father for a favored son. Joseph's coat of many colors was gone now, moth-eaten and tossed out during spring cleaning one May afternoon years after Joseph's death. This ground only remained, and Joseph's adventurous life of betrayal and slavery and a rise to royalty in a strange place was reduced to a few pages of scripture. In that idle moment by Jacob's well, Jesus had gotten his wish and forgotten where he was coming from and where he was going. Only this time and place remained, a time and place full of reminders that all of a person's days come down to one lonely moment, to this lonely moment in a strange place. All his life was a lonely moment before death—a death toward which each instant of his life pointed from his birth in a manger to his hearing the water in Jacob's well.

"It was about noon" (John 4:6), the story goes, and you hear a clock ticking somewhere in the darkness of your home. It was a moment in time, and all hours or even all years before that could have been ticks of the clock. Like the darkness surrounding you in your hallway at night, the heat of the sun was the weight of a cross on Jesus' shoulders, and he was thirsty. On another day in the not-so-distant future, the noon hour would be the hour when an otherwise insignificant Roman governor would stir and pour water over his hands and turn Jesus over to a mob, to a real cross (John 19:14). It would happen on another day, in another tick of the clock, in the twinkling of the sun's reflection on well water.

Today, however, the sound of water stirring and pouring was a sound of life if ever there was life in a thirsty man. Jesus turned and saw the lone woman drawing water from the well, making sounds of baptism with the water as surely as John the Baptist and Jesus' disciples made sounds of baptism, sounds of death to the world and of a new life beyond the ticking of the clock, beyond moments of death like this moment. Jesus was a fugitive in a strange land because his disciples made sounds of baptism under the noses of Pharisees who ran out of town any challenger to their monopoly on the way to life and death. With an alien fugitive's eyes, he saw the woman's face as she gently worked the water, and he saw in her face eyes unadjusted to light as she strained to see in the sun's glare. Just under her nose where she could almost taste it, water in human form stirred, water she had drawn all her passing days to sustain her life, water with life so familiar that she could scarcely recognize the wonder of it.

"Give me a drink," he requested of her, and the silence that followed was the sound of a waterfall stopping, as the woman and the earth beneath her feet and the air she breathed were stunned that any man spoke to her at all. Her sense of shock followed not from who he was but from who she was: A woman so convinced that she was a lost cause that she married and divorced five lost causes. A woman who never married for the right reason because, even if she knew the right reason, she had no doubt that it was too right for one as unworthy as her. She was a Samaritan woman addressed by a Jew in an age when Jews considered themselves too good to take a dime from a Samaritan, much less a drink of water. As a woman, she was forbidden company to a Jewish rabbi, and worse yet, she considered herself forbidden company to any man or anything smacking of holiness. She saw her reflection in Jacob's well, her face spent with use and abuse, with eyes unaccustomed to light and more accustomed to the darkness which dogged her even in the glaring sunlight of that moment.

Just as she felt ashamed before men and Jews and religion, she felt a healthy dose of anger at men and Jews and religion, enough anger at least to break the stunned silence by outdoing Jesus himself at speaking the unspeakable—since it was unspeakable for her to speak at all. "How is it that you, a Jew, ask a drink of me, a woman of Samaria?" Water spilled from her ladle back into the well. The sound of water splashing on water. The sun playing in the ripples in Jacob's well. The tick of a clock. All her life, her five failed marriages and her five thousand losses and her fifty-five thousand disappointed hopes condensed into one glittering droplet of water that rebounded upward from the splash and soaked unnoticed into her sleeve. All her life somehow led up to the breaking of silence, the ticking of a clock, the splashing of water, and this stranger gave her the vague, uncomfortable sense that this moment was her last bittersweet moment before a kind of death, a kind of life. So she sought refuge in reminding him who he was (a Jew) and who she was (a Samaritan and a woman) and hoped that they could then return to business as usual.

"If you knew the gift of God, and who it is that is saying to you, 'Give me a drink,' you would have asked him, and he would have given you living water," Jesus responded, knowing full well that she knew who it was asking her for a drink. She knew who he was, but she could not admit to herself that she could know anyone as full of life and hope as a messiah. But she could know a messiah better than most because in all of her suffering and humiliation and failed hopes she knew she could not believe in anything less than a messiah. She could not be swayed by any false messiahs because she knew their come-on lines, having followed all of them and having been burned every time. Moreover, she could recognize a messiah because she was a kind of messiah herself, "despised and rejected . . . as one from whom others hide their faces" as Isaiah prophesied (Isa. 53:3), speaking the universal language of suffering with the look on her face,

speaking the universal language of life as she made the
sound of water, stirring and pouring at Jacob's well. Jesus
knew that she recognized him before she knew it herself.

In a tick of the clock, she asked the lonely, thirsty rabbi
who he was, and in another tick he told her that he sup-
plies a kind of water that quenches thirst forevermore,
that brings rest and refreshment to the sleepless, that
brings a kind of love which five or five thousand divorces
cannot contaminate, that takes the small droplet of life
remaining in the moment of death and makes of it an
ocean that washes death away. In another tick of the
clock, she listened to this wonderful stranger describe her
past in just a passing utterance, in just a droplet of time
and memory, as if he had been with her all along. As the
sounds of his disciples' footsteps and animated whispers
signaled their return, he told her of a time so vast and a
truth so wet with life that it would overflow the borders
of Israel. God would brood over the waters of time and
truth and over her spirit and old Jacob's spirit and every
estranged Samaritan's spirit with a motherly love that
would not let them die.

With Jesus' turn to meet his returning disciples, you
awaken, two thousand years from him or only an instant,
in the present, your bathrobe wrinkled and your hair on
one side of your head, your eyes seeing better in the darkness. The refrigerator door remains closed, the motor
humming. You remember your day again—the faces, the
sounds, the high pulse, the splashing of tap water on your
face. You remember your life again—the work and play,
loving and burying those you love, every kind of baptism
and divorce that come with the ebb and flow of the tide.
The memory becomes an utterance of Christ, a droplet of
water splashing into a sea of living water that never evap-
orates, that washes away death. The clock ticks.

CHAPTER 18

Rush Hour

What gain have the workers from their toil? I have seen
the business that God has given to everyone to be busy
with. He has made everything suitable for its time; moreover he has put a sense of past and future into their minds,
yet they cannot find out what God has done from the
beginning to the end.

Ecclesiastes 3:9–11

During early morning rush hour on the interstate, my
eyes are a contradiction of sluggishness and vigilance as I
survey the highway filled with fellow maniacs. I drive an
old, faded-blue Datsun station wagon, license number
PMB-918. The lady in OGV-762 applies mascara at 67
miles per hour. The gentleman in MT-1992 artfully bal-
ances a cup of coffee while changing lanes to escape the
blue exhaust from a half-dead Fairlane. AXW-011, a
bright-red Honda sports car with tinted glass and no apparent driver, weaves wildly past, disappearing in the
black haze left by the three 18-wheelers it passed in no
time flat. Across the divide, nobody can hear the siren
over the chatter of morning deejays, and an ambulance is
forced to brake. Spitting and hissing at the white Conti-
nental ahead that slowed me to 58 miles per hour, I glance
around insanely and whip my car into an open lane like a
bad guy in a chase scene.

If the tenuous choreography of the traffic is disrupted
by so much as the sneeze of a driver with a clumsy grip
on the steering wheel, we will die in the chaotic careening
of cars. If we are lucky, we will survive for now and die a

more professionally monitored death years later in the cardiac unit of the hospital to which the medical technologist in ABT-885 rushes. This brink-of-death madness called rush hour is an orchestrated expression of "chasing the wind," a theme that my backseat driver, Koheleth, develops in the book of Ecclesiastes.

The basic thrust of Ecclesiastes is that all our efforts amount to vanity, tilting at windmills, chasing the wind, or in a word, rush-hour traffic. No matter how fast we go or how artfully we dodge, "under the sun the race is not to the swift, nor the battle to the strong, nor bread to the wise, nor riches to the intelligent, nor favor to the skillful; but time and chance happen to them all" (Eccl. 9:11). Not exactly the positive thinker's creed. Furthermore, no matter how safely one drives here and there, one ultimately arrives at the same destination as the drunk driver: the graveyard. Meanwhile, in God's inevitable and unknowable plan, whether one comes out a winner or a loser is totally a matter of divine caprice.

Koheleth's book of Ecclesiastes somehow managed to win a place in the Bible, but I would not recommend him as a guest speaker at vacation church school. Yet I suffer from a peculiar attraction to strange birds like Koheleth, so I let him come along with me for the rush-hour ride.

Koheleth slouches in my backseat talking. In the rearview mirror, I see his fleshy face and dark, baggy eyes. He watches cars constantly, his expression varying from a smug, superior smile to sneering disgust to wet-eyed pity, depending, I suppose, on the driver's face he happens to be watching or on the ebb and flow of his moods. Koheleth is a snob, he is stinking rich, he is a drunk, and sometimes I don't know why I put up with him. For all his complaining that nobody deserves his inheritance when he dies, I wonder why he plays at being chauffeur-driven in my clunker when he is perfectly capable of hiring a real chauffeur. Sometimes I speculate that he takes some perverse pleasure or pain in watching me in action, one of the fools of the world who creates and fights rush-hour traffic.

Just when I am about to drop him off at a Mercedes dealer and tell him to buy his own car and drive himself home, that look of pity crosses his eyes. His voice cracks as he continues his discourse on the vanity and futility of rush hour. It occurs to me as he sadly complains of seeing "solitary individuals, without sons or brothers" (Eccl. 4:8), that he is taking many glances at his own reflection in my rearview mirror. Then I recant, concluding that he comes along for the maddening ride because in rush-hour traffic, as he watches the empty-eyed drivers barrel and weave for no apparent reason, he communes with his own kind.

So I listen to his rambling theology of futility and fate: "We have cars! Ha-ha! Congratulations, humankind! Now we can carry on with our foolishness faster, and we can accomplish more emptiness in more places in the course of a day. Why, in my day, we would go nowhere slowly, on mule or camel or on the backs of our slaves. But this rocketing about in cars, ha-ha! This is futility with a vengeance!

"What?" he continues as if I said something. "You call the invention of cars and planes and trash mashers and televisions and VCRs and Touch-Tone phones progress? I tell you all these technological advances are just new forms of chasing the wind. But enjoy them now, for later you will die just as we did in the days when chasing the wind was a more primitive art."

He takes a few loud swallows from a brown bag, burps politely, and carries on, "I suppose you have never asked yourself whether you chase the wind in all your endeavors. Believe me, you're not alone. If everybody seriously asked that question, nobody would see any point in going anywhere, and there would be nobody on this highway right now.

"Look at the fellow driving the Pontiac to your right. His face is a blank mask, he is in a mindless trance. The poor wretch has to believe in some purpose, some design to his driving in this madness, to his toiling eight, nine, ten hours a day at the Savings and Loan, to his weekend worry over the health of his lawn; otherwise, he could scarcely make sense of his life. He would be too unsettled to watch his Sunday football game on the tube. In order to spare this man from too much discomfort, God, with infinite mercy, permits fanatics in the end zones to hold up signs reading 'John 3:16' but never 'Ecclesiastes 3:16!' " Koheleth laughs long and low, then hysterically when I remind him with a reluctant grin that not many people in a football stadium can spell "Ecclesiastes" anyway.

The laughter dies down, and he sits silently for a while. I glance in the rearview mirror and see him cast a long, pitying gaze toward the poor slob in the Pontiac. A few minutes more and I glance again to find him staring at himself in my mirror with the same bleeding look. He catches my eye and speaks with a sudden sadness, "I suppose I am too much of a 'results man' who must have *full* satisfaction *now* for my work and worry or I'm *never* satisfied. I've made a life of despairing over inequities and uncertainties, over never having quite enough money or luck or good times to sit back and just feel . . . blessed, I suppose. Yes, I make all the noise over going ahead and enjoying wine, women, and song while we can. But I can't be satisfied, or else I never would have written Ecclesiastes. I can't seem to rise above the very foolishness that I point out so well.

"I don't know if you noticed, but when I wrote Ecclesiastes, I was angry at God. I scarcely realized it myself at the time, but it's there in the text with my sarcastic allusions to how God, who carries on the real business of life, merely busies us with our empty pursuits. Concealing the only designs and purposes that really count, the Lord promises hidden mercy now and a vague eternal life later, but keeps us guessing about just what our trifling means and ends have to do with it all. God gives old Koheleth the gift of seeing the futility but not the gift of seeing the meaning, the point of it all. Leaves me in my stew.

"God said to the prophets, 'Go,' and they went, and all sorts of signs and wonders and ironies came to light. Jesus said to his disciples, 'Follow me,' and they followed, confused, bungling to the bitter end, and they saw victory over death. Christ says to old Koheleth, 'Come,' and I reply, 'Where?' And he just walks, dammit, expecting me to follow. So I follow, but not right behind him because I don't want him to know I'm there. I follow incognito, on a parallel road just out of sight, or in a distant crowd where there are too many faces to make out mine. I lurk in nearby bars and smoke-filled rooms where a Christ would never set foot but where I can keep tabs on him. But then, dammit, he comes in to the bar and gives me that look that practically says, 'Welcome to my bar,' and all I can do is smile sheepishly back at him.

"Why do I come along for the ride each morning, pestering, taunting, ridiculing, drinking like a fish? Because I know he's just ahead, somewhere on this Godforsaken road. How do I know? Because there are hitchhikers and little old ladies who drive too fearfully slow down the exit ramps. Because there's a guy late for work who needs desperately to get into the right lane. Because there's a lady in an expensive dress trying to change a tire and a pale fellow in an old pickup getting browbeaten by a state trooper. Because there's the guy in the Pontiac who is so numb with pain and boredom that he can hardly see straight. Because in all this rush-hour madness I constantly find subtle interludes from suffering people, and where suffering people are, Christ is there, suffering. So as I ride with you, I follow Christ and get as close as I can to him without actually getting close enough to touch him or to let him see me."

Koheleth wept softly for the remainder of our ride. When we reached our destination, I invited him to come along for the next ride, which startled him because previously he always came uninvited. I also thanked him, which startled us both at the time because neither of us quite knew what I had to thank him for. But now I know. I thanked him for the glimpse of Christ he gave in my rearview mirror.

CHAPTER 19

The Raging Love of Mother Mary

> Meanwhile, standing near the cross of Jesus were his mother, and his mother's sister, Mary the wife of Clopas, and Mary Magdalene. When Jesus saw his mother and the disciple whom he loved standing beside her, he said to his mother, "Woman, here is your son." Then he said to the disciple, "Here is your mother." And from that hour the disciple took her into his own home.
>
> *John 19:25–27*

"My God, my God, why have you forsaken me?" Mary heard her oldest son, Jesus, cry out from the cross (Mark 15:34). The cry echoed in the dark sky about his bloody, suspended body. The cry echoed in a dark emptiness in the pit of her being, an emptiness he left there since his birth, an emptiness he could never fill because he was always too caught up in his urgent, brutal, holy task to be her son.

Jesus cried out, and for a moment even the hecklers hushed, even the swaggering Roman guards hesitated and glanced over their shoulders at her broken son. His cry of Godforsakenness posed a question some of them could remember hearing in the muffled groans of their own hearts, but they never heard the question spoken aloud before, much less cried out amid the bustling, grunting masses and into God's heaven. In that hushed moment, everyone there believed that the cross brought on that unspeakable question.

Everyone but Mary, of course, who was with Jesus for the initial forsakenness in a drafty stable with her nervous, exhausted husband. Delirious, wild-eyed, over-worked shepherds came swearing that they heard something, saw something or somebody who led them there. Mary knew that the forsakenness began there as she held her firstborn boy in the least likely imaginable birthplace for a king. She knew that the forsakenness be-gan with the birth, not the crucifixion, of her little one, her Jesus, now nailed to a tree with his life flashing before his eyes.

She knew his cry of forsakenness was thirty-three years in coming, and if all anyone would ever remember of him was his sordid death, she at least would remember the birth and the lonely misunderstood years of her son's life. Not that she understood it, this life preceded by heav-enly messages of promise and hope and outright glory, but which played itself out in tiring treks down dusty roads from one swarming mass of broken, salvation-starved people to another.

Jesus' words of the kingdom, of his kingship, grabbed the heart but tragically eluded the understanding. Hearts closed and hardened again with the passing of a few days. He spoke of death as if it were the only hope, and here he was dying in a midday darkness, no hope in sight, crying out in Godforsakenness.

Mary wiped her tears and clenched her jaw as a wave of anger rose in her, filling her up. This was not anger at Rome or tired, befuddled Pilate. This was not anger at the religious authorities who arranged Jesus' death. Judas could hang. She would not waste her anger on him. Nor was this anger at the other disciples who scattered like hens when the Roman guard and Judas descended like foxes upon Jesus in Gethsemane. No, this was not anger at the liars and fools who made her son's sordid death possi-ble. This was anger at her dying son himself, Jesus.

If Jesus was Godforsaken, she thought, she was sonfor-saken. From the moment of his weaning until his betrayal and persecution, the glory of God the Father so preoccu-pied him that he overlooked his lowly mother, the handmaid of the Lord. Never mind that she was chosen too. Never mind that, in a sense, they were in this together, this incarnation.

When Joseph and she took their twelve-year-old son to Jerusalem, Jesus made himself scarce in the Temple while they searched frantically for three days. When they finally found him shooting the breeze with some dried-up, Bible-thumping Temple scholars in a back room, he responded to her scolding by saying that he was surprised that she cared and by reminding her that he really belonged there, not with her. She would have slapped his face but for the rightness of the look in his eyes and the admiration in the eyes of the teachers in the room.

The Godforsakenness of Jesus began with his birth during a census. He was an anonymous number from the start, and it seemed that he blamed her for that, retaliating by never calling her "mother," but always "woman." "Woman, what have you to do with me?" (John 2:4, RSV) he mumbled at a wedding early in his short career when she informed him that the drinks were running low and would he please perform one of his little miracles. Later, when someone notified him that she had arrived for one of his speaking engagements, he asked, "Who is my mother?" (Matt. 12:48) and announced that everyone else there, assuming they do his Father's will, is his mother.

Yes, they were in this together, Mary realized angrily as her first son felt the weight of death on his cold, torn shoulders. But what they were in together was not what she expected, not the glory of God, it seemed, but common forsakenness: he, forsaken by the God he could not keep his eyes off of, and she, forsaken by the son whom she still loved as the apple of her eye in spite of her better judgment. Now with his dying, with his leaving her without so much as acknowledging her as his mother, a forsaken rage filled that emptiness her son never bothered to fill before it was too late.

Then he looked at her. She could not recall that look since her infant son's puffy eyes first opened and looked into her eyes as if to call her Mother. Now, without speaking, he seemed to say from the cross, "If nothing else makes sense in this world for me, the newborn one, the dying one, the one born to die, at least here is my mother. And she loves me. I know it because she is here. The only thing that would be right in this very wrong world would be for her to hold me. But she can't. At least not until I am dead."

Mary stepped toward her son. As she walked, she took on a new face, or rather an old face, the face of the virgin looking into her newborn son's eyes for the first time. This seemed to all the world like a walk from life into the darkness of death, but mother and son knew somehow that it was something quite different, a walk from death into the arms of life. When she could see the color in her firstborn's eyes, she stopped. In the silence of their gazing, mother and son understood each other, both forsaken by the ones to whom they gave their lives but both strangely aware that there was more time left, more than either of them could imagine for her to be the mother and he, the Son.

Jesus shifted his gaze slightly to her side, and she noticed his most beloved disciple standing next to her. This was the young one, deerlike, with gentle, sad eyes, always lovable for his untarnished and simple desire to love and be loved. Yet, in all his innocence, he always seemed more than the others to quietly, deeply understand her son, who he was and what he was about, even now in all the boy's grief over the suffering of his Lord and friend.

Mary looked back up at Jesus who looked down at her, and for less than an instant his dying eyes shone. "Woman," he called her for the last painful time, nodding toward his disciple, "Behold, your son." She remembered the first time she heard those words, Joseph's first words moments after Jesus was born in that drafty stable, spoken with a breathless voice and white, trembling lips. Shepherds spoke those words too, startled and awestruck as if they sought a lost lamb in the brush and found God.

A short time later, wise and peculiar travelers with misty eyes and shaggy eyebrows spoke those words in whispers filled with wonder as if she had given birth to the very star they followed to that place. Elderly Simeon and Anna spoke those words as if they lived their many years just to see this little one's face. Now the child himself spoke those words to Mary with his dying breaths.

Jesus looked squarely at the beloved disciple and said, "Behold, your mother." His voice echoed in the dark sky about him and in the dark space left in her soul from a lifetime of not hearing him call her his mother. This gift, a living son who looked at her with eyes that seemed to call her Mother was a gift only God could give, and somehow she knew that this beloved disciple was the grace she had waited for all these years.

This gift quieted her rage but did not quell it. Mary walked to the foot of the cross hoping Jesus, her Jesus, would somehow live, hoping against hope that he would call her Mother, *his* mother. Yet, as her firstborn son breathed his last and her new son comforted her, that strange hope remained in her angry, loving heart. It was a hope that Jesus' death would not be the last word, that his love for her would not be silenced forever. It was a hope that could never die, a hope so strong that it was a prayer she prayed just by hoping. A prayer that God could not help but answer.

CHAPTER 20

The Cry of
the Shepherd Boy

The king was deeply moved, and went up to the chamber
over the gate, and wept; and as he went, he said, "O my
son Absalom, my son, my son Absalom! Would I had died
instead of you, O Absalom, my son, my son!"

2 Samuel 18:33

On a sweltering midsummer afternoon near the gates of
his encampment, King David sat sweating under an um-
brella. Humidity seemed more than enough to account for
his drenched royal garments, but anxiety accounted for
his perspiration even more. David wiped his face and
neck with towel after towel, seeing no point in retreating
to a cooler place because there was no escaping this anxiety. He kept his eyes on the gate, waiting for news more
vital to his slowly breaking heart than to his kingdom
teetering in the balance.

Somewhere over the horizon David's troops fought the
decisive battle of a civil war. Once Israel's mightiest war-
rior, the old battle-ax nursed his arthritic knees, swatted
mosquitoes, and tried to look calm as he waited for news
from the front. David knew the Lord would deliver again,
that his side would win. But no nightmare could be
darker even than victory in this war, for the leader of the
revolt was Absalom, his own son.

Youth. What David would give to win it back. When he
was a boy tending sheep, being a king was a fanciful
dream and finding a lost lamb brought as much elation as
any victory in battle ever could. He remembered the
sounds of sheep grazing and their sudden, gentle calls to

no one in particular. David would sing out himself sometimes just for God and sky and sheep to hear. He remembered the wind in the grass, the feel of his fingers on the harp, the sound of the brook which he imitated with music.

Then fantasy became reality. Dreaming innocence erupted into conquest and power and dance. His father, Jesse, called him out of the fields one day to meet a tired, bent old prophet named Samuel who stood glowering at a lineup of David's seven older brothers. Samuel looked at David, squinted and contorted his lips as if eating a bad fig, spit on the ground, and looked back up at David with admiration that the boy would see again and again for decades to come upon thousands of faces. Samuel anointed David king on the spot even as Saul reigned.

The boy shepherd rose to power in rapid and charmed steps. He soothed King Saul's deteriorating mind with music and song. He slayed a giant and became Israel's darling overnight. As King Saul's lunacy became homicidal jealousy, David eluded death like a fox. In the end, Saul only succeeded in killing himself, and David cleaned up Israel's foes in battle. Like magic, the boy shepherd was now the boy king. If youth ever charmed the heart of God himself, it happened the day young King David and his men brought home the long lost symbol of their faith, the ark of the covenant. David danced all but naked at the head of a ticker-tape parade through the streets of Jerusalem with trumpets blowing and crowds cheering for the glory of God, David, and youth itself.

Now the king was over the hill, and Absalom, his son, was youth, the youth that captured the heart and imagination of the whole nation and his father most of all. David remembered his son as a baby, and if winning over the king's heart wins the kingdom, then Absalom won the kingdom with his first step and secured it forever with his first word. David remembered his son, all long legs and bright, brown saucer eyes and freckles and flowing hair, running to greet his father when he returned from

battle, keeping David up well into the night with questions about the latest victory. Absalom grew tall and muscular and secretive as adolescent boys do, and David
knew his aloofness was his way of retreating into lonely
places like young David did as a shepherd boy, places
where boys dream and find their own secret music.

Then David lost touch with Absalom as he lost touch
with God and kingdom and music in the aftermath of his
almost perfect, sordid crime. He lost touch with youth at
the same time. The last time David truly felt young, he
looked casually from the roof of his house and saw Bathsheba, the wife of his faithful trooper Uriah. She was
bathing, and her shapely body, her clear, glistening skin,
her cascading, jet black locks of hair, and her face of soft
grace drove him mad with youth and hunger.

Like clockwork, he arranged a sexual liaison with Bathsheba, which she could not dare refuse the king, God's
anointed one. She became pregnant. He managed to cover
up the affair and secure Bathsheba for his concubine by
arranging her husband Uriah's death in an impossible
battle assignment. No mortal could detect his perfect
crime.

But the same shepherd boy who sang out to God in
green pastures, knowing that God watched and reveled in
his every move, forgot, as king, that God still watched.
When the prophet Nathan reminded David that God was
still watching and knew what David had done, David re-
pented with such heartfelt, mournful music that surely
even Uriah's ghost forgave him, not to mention the God of
grace. But the mourning of the shepherd boy did not
reach its anguished crescendo until months later when his
first child by Bathsheba died at seven days old.

David was forgiven, but he was never the same again.
He grew stodgy, restless, preoccupied, always half there
at best. He became a royal procrastinator, stopped listening with more than one ear to his advisers, forgot to pray,
forgot the music. He kept to himself and did not mind the
shop. His children grew older without him as he sat

closed up in his chamber, drinking wine, reminiscing, staring out the window.

Absalom sensed his father's absence, and he became an angry young man determined to make the whole kingdom give him their love if his father had none left to give. As David looked the other way, scandal after scandal infested not only the kingdom but the king's own family, and Absalom took it upon himself to set things straight. Soon Absalom's rage grew against his father's neglect, and his rage became a terrible beauty that the absent king's subjects loved. Absalom's long, flowing hair became a symbol of youth in all its wildness, fury, and hunger, and half the kingdom rallied around their new prince of youth in open rebellion. As the world spun around the tired, perplexed king, Israel's Camelot collapsed.

So David sat nervously under the blazing sun, remembering youth, remembering Absalom, his son. The king had given strict orders that the war was to be won but Absalom spared, taken alive so father and son could work things out. But David could not remember to whom he had given those orders or whether he said it right. He was not much good at getting the details right anymore, much less remembering them. His heart was out there on the battlefield, exposed, helpless, hunted, with nowhere to turn. He wiped his brow, coughed, sipped water, and tried to smile.

Then the watchman called, "King David, a solitary man runs toward us." David's heart was a desperate fugitive pounding a stranger's door. "If he runs alone, he brings good news," the king pronounced, bargaining with fate. Before the messenger arrived, the watchman announced, "See, another man running alone!" an added confusion cast aside with David's wishful reply, "He too must bring good news."

The first messenger dashed through the gate. David stood up, and the breathless messenger looked as David felt, his eyes wide and wild, his skin flushed. He screeched, "All is well!" David, his veins standing out in his neck, his right cheek twitching, demanded, "What about Absalom?" The messenger sputtered some garbled evasion, threw up his hands, shrugged his shoulders, and tried to die. "Stand here quietly," David ordered with the eerie, trembling hush of dying words.

The next messenger strode in with confidence, a knowing twinkle in his eye. In a grandiose tone, he announced, "Good tidings for my lord the king! For the LORD has vindicated you this day, delivering you from the power of all who rose up against you." His heart near the breaking point, David asked, "Is it well with the young man Absalom?" If the first messenger's idiocy could be outdone, the second one did it, obviously not realizing that he was talking about the apple of his lord the king's eye, "May the enemies of my lord the king, and all who rise up to do you harm, be like that young man" (2 Sam. 18:24–32).

Absalom was dead.

At that moment, far away in a meadow where David the boy shepherd once tended sheep and dreamed and found music by the brook, there were no sheep, no shepherd boys: Only grass and birds and minnows and creatures of the earth. And God. The God who still watched that place. The God who remembered the shepherd boy's call into the sky just for the joy of being there, being alive, being at all. Now God heard in that faraway place the shepherd boy cry, "O my son Absalom, my son, my son Absalom! Would I had died instead of you, O Absalom, my son, my son!"

God departed from that lonely meadow and went to a place even more lonely, to the grieving king. God remained with David as the long, sorrowful days and sleepless nights passed. God was with him in his lonely chamber as the victorious but inconsolable king sat in the blackness of bereavement, punctuating the groaning silence with angry epithets at God and long, ponderous sighs. God waited. Then David, almost without forethought, stood up one day, walked to his desk, and wrote a brief psalm:

O Lord, my heart is not lifted up,
   my eyes are not raised too high;
I do not occupy myself with things
   too great and too marvelous for me.
But I have calmed and quieted my soul,
   like a weaned child with its mother;
   my soul is like the weaned child that is with me.

O Israel, hope in the Lord
   from this time on and forevermore.

(Psalm 131)

God loved David with a motherly love deeper than it had been for the innocent shepherd boy, a love wider than it had been for the dancing young king. God remained with King David forevermore.

CHAPTER 21

Daddy's Nightmare

[Jesus said,] "Whoever comes to me and does not hate father and mother, wife and children, brothers and sisters,
yes, and even life itself, cannot be my disciple."

Luke 14:26

Then they seized him and led him away, bringing him
into the high priest's house. But Peter was following at a
distance. When they had kindled a fire in the middle of
the courtyard and sat down together, Peter sat among
them. Then a servant-girl, seeing him in the firelight,
stared at him and said, "This man also was with him."
But he denied it, saying, "Woman, I do not know him." A
little later someone else, on seeing him, said, "You also are
one of them." But Peter said, "Man, I am not!" Then about
an hour later still another kept insisting, "Surely this man
also was with him; for he is a Galilean." But Peter said,
"Man, I do not know what you are talking about!" At that
moment, while he was still speaking, the cock crowed.

Luke 22:54–60

It is the children's bedtime in a typical middle-class suburban home. The collie patrols the fenced-in backyard for
suspicious odors and sounds, and the streetlights illumi-
nate the front yard like a midsummer night in Alaska,
enabling neighbors and police to detect suspicious characters. The air conditioner keeps the whole house at room
temperature, the bedsheets are clean and soft, and all is
safe and comfortable in this typical home on this typical
night during this typical week.

Of course, there are two children, a girl and a boy, ages five and three, Suzy and Johnny. After a failure at doing cartwheels with his sister in the den, Johnny cries like a child who has fallen through a manhole and into the arms of Satan. As Daddy carries him on his shoulders, he stops crying, sniffing and giggling through the house, as Mommy redirects Suzy from cartwheels to a sober discussion of what to wear in the morning. Children and Daddy then converge in the den for bedtime stories as Mommy says her good nights and goes to the back of the house to fold towels.

As a typical businessman in a typical town, Daddy is a churchgoing Christian. Lately, he reads to the children from the Bible at bedtime, not because he expects them to understand very much of it, but because he wants them to get into the habit of paying attention to the Bible each day. Daddy reads from Luke, the Gospel in which Jesus prays often and has compassion for little people like children, but he makes the mistake of reading from the unedited grown-up version. He picks a spot in the middle of Luke and reads in a monotone, the children's eyes getting heavier, his own eyes getting heavier. Then Daddy reaches this sentence, a direct quote from gentle Jesus, and reads it aloud without forethought, "Whoever comes to me and does not hate father and mother, wife and children, brothers and sisters, yes, and even life itself, cannot be my disciple."

Suddenly all eyes open wide, all pupils dilate, and there is some explaining to do. The children aren't stupid. They know what "hate" means, and they have probably already done their fair share of hating in their brief time on this planet. Little Suzy asks, "Can I hate Johnny for pulling my hair when Jesus says I can?"

Daddy must make haste before this situation gets out of control and the children decide that they have license to kill. "Umm, well, S-Suzy"—he furrows his moist brow wisely—"it was very important to Jesus that we love him with all our heart, and all our soul, and all our mind. It was so important to him that sometimes he exaggerated to make his point." Johnny, who cannot possibly know what Daddy means, looks reassured. For Suzy's sake, Daddy continues, "In this passage, Jesus is trying to tell us that we should love him so much that we love him more than we love anybody else, including our mommies and daddies and brothers and sisters. He does not really mean that we should not love our parents and brothers and sisters, but he said 'hate' just to startle us and make us pay attention. And it worked, didn't it?" Daddy beams a beleaguered smile.

Having sedated them with an explanation, Daddy makes them sing to really knock them out, "Jesus loves me! This I know, for the Bible tells me so. . . . " All sing along, Suzy smiles again, and Johnny is in a pious stupor. Daddy polishes them off with a group prayer, "Now I lay me down to sleep . . . ," takes them to their rooms, and tucks them in. Then he snatches the Bible up from the coffee table in the den, swears under his breath that he'll never let his children near it again, and marches straight to the kitchen for a snack and a closer look.

Milk trickles down Daddy's chin as he checks the footnote for Luke 14:26 and finds Matthew 10:37 in barely perceptible fine print, the cross-reference that might restore the foundation of his life as a daddy and husband and even son. Madly turning back the pages with his left hand, he wipes the milk from his chin with his right sleeve, knocking over his glass of milk with his elbow. Oblivious to milk flowing swiftly across the table and cascading to the floor, he finds the crucial cross-reference and reads, "Whoever loves father or mother more than me is not worthy of me; and whoever loves son or daughter more than me is not worthy of me" (Matt. 10:37).

A short-lived sense of relief comes over him as he realizes that he explained the passage correctly to his children. Then Mommy enters and intervenes, "So what level of the animal kingdom have we descended to when we loll around in our own spilled milk with no concept of cleaning it up?" Only semiconscious of her presence and, again, without forethought, Daddy blandly replies, "I am looking for biblical assurance that I should not hate my wife." Suddenly there is more explaining to do.

Two hours later, Daddy and Mommy have argued and kissed and made up like young lovers. Daddy brushes his teeth, checks the locks, takes a peek at the children, and joins Mommy in bed. Soon after their nightly cuddling and talking ritual, she is on the other side of the bed, and Daddy listens to her breathing get longer and louder as he stares intently into the darkness.

Luke's "hate your family" passage will not go away in spite of Matthew's reassuring version of it. He sees it on the thin white page of the Bible. He hears himself read it aloud and feels the frustration and shock over the words that just came out of his mouth. He sees the children's eyes. There in his comfortable and secure home, with the locks locked and the central air conditioning quietly cooling the rooms, with the rituals of bedtime and marriage, an unemployed carpenter with callused, dusty feet and no wife or kids and no roof over his head at night intrudes, leaving Daddy feeling as though something is undone. Daddy searches the darkness for a clue to some forgotten act, a forgotten ritual of cross-bearing, a forgotten habit of discipleship that he must have overlooked as he and Mommy established the rituals of their family.

Daddy thinks of Peter, the only disciple he can remember this late at night. Surely Peter did not hate his family. Like Daddy, Peter tended to talk before thinking. When Jesus prophesied his own death, Peter tried to launder his boss's words, only to get kicked in the butt by him. That is how Daddy feels—kicked in the butt.

At least Daddy never denied Jesus like Peter did three times when Jesus needed him most. What I did could have been a lot worse, Daddy thinks with a smile, awkwardly casting aside his guilty ruminations. Call it denial, call it rationalization, call it a cop-out. It works. At least it works long enough for Daddy's mind to unwind, for him to listen to the slow rhythm of Mommy's breathing, for his mind to drift to pleasant childhood memories of his mother and his brother, and before he can get to his father, he allows himself the gift of sleep. With sleep, there comes a dream:

The night is hot, the steamy air almost too thick to breathe. Daddy lights up another cigarette, having scarcely taken a breath all day without a smoke. He paces back and forth in an alley he shares with a few rats scurrying among overflowing garbage cans. The adjacent street is abuzz with talk of a gadfly Galilean, a magical healer, a king of the Jews. Bets are placed on who sent him, what he really wanted, how long it will take him to die, whether he will pull another miracle because everyone is quite certain that the Romans will crucify him in order to appease the most religious citizens of this most religious city, Jerusalem.

Daddy knows the man of whom they speak. Daddy left his home and fishing trade three years back to follow this man, and it did not take long before Daddy called this man his teacher. Daddy was the first to call him the Christ, the promised one of Israel, and though his teacher warned Daddy and all witnesses not to refer to him as Christ outside that circle, now all the people on the street refer to him, in most cases sarcastically, as the promised Messiah. The title is now among the main reasons that Daddy's teacher is condemned to die.

Daddy, however, knows the man not only as teacher and Christ. He knows the sight and smell of the sweat on his back as they walked the roads from town to town. He knows the feel of his teacher's rough fingers washing Daddy's feet. Daddy knows the sound of his teacher's voice calling to him over the waves in a dark night on the sea. He has seen all of humankind in his teacher's eyes: the ferocious intensity, the wet-eyed compassion, the mischievous laughter, the distant, bereft look. Daddy has followed this teacher, this Christ, for three years, walking with him until it seemed that there was no walking without him. The man has called Daddy his rock one minute and Satan himself the next, and Daddy has sworn that he would die for this man, this man of whom the people murmur on the street tonight.

For the first time in three years, Daddy is away from the rest of the poor slobs who left their lives behind to follow an unemployed carpenter who did not have a bed to sleep on but who promised that all the treasure you could ever want is back home in his Father's basement. For once, Daddy can stop and reflect and take stock of this mad venture, and, who knows, maybe he can write it off as temporary insanity or his "religious phase of life" and go back home. He can fish again: Real fish. Fish that thrash about in the nets and fill the air with spray and the salty green smell of the deep. Fish that sell at the markets as long as people have stomachs to fill. Fish you can fry by the lake for breakfast in the early morning as the mist clears.

Perhaps the time has come to abandon this fishing for people, people who greet you like a prince one day and plot your crucifixion the next. Maybe Daddy can go back home and fish and, next time religion calls, follow his wife instead of a savior. She will not uproot him like a weed. She will let him fish, and he will be a father. His children will love him like children and rebel like fools and finally love him like adults. Daddy can grow old and die quietly in his own small, unbothered kingdom.

He walks to the street, takes the last drag from his cigarette and stamps it out. Briefly, he surveys the street as he inserts another cigarette between his lips and lights a match. As he cups his hands over the cigarette to light it, the pale glow of the match's flame exposes his face for all nearby night prowlers to see. Out of the shadows a coarse, slurring female voice screeches, "I've seen you! You are one of his men!"

Daddy shakes out the match and hides his face in smoke. "What? Me? What are you talking about?" he responds with a quick choke. As the woman approaches him from the shadows, he sees her face, his own mother's face, but without his mother's milky optimism or calming voice. Just a smirk chiseled into her wrinkles from a lifetime of cynical leering on a dog-eat-dog street.

She continues, "You're one of his men, the traveling healer from Nazareth. Will you carry on his trade after they've nailed him up? Did he teach you big-league healing, like blindness or leprosy? How about the common cold? Could you help me get over my sniffles?"

She doubles over and quakes and howls with a long mocking laugh as a small crowd gathers, the drunker ones joining her in laughing into his smoke. He chuckles quietly along, "I've never seen any such healing, but if you find a wonderful doctor like that, introduce me to him. I have a few aches and pains I'd like for him to check out."

From his blind side to the left, Daddy hears his own brother's voice speaking with uncharacteristic tenderness, "I know you were with him, and I just want to know how I can help." Daddy turns and sees a tall robed figure with a hood casting a shadow over his bandaged face, his eyes peeking out from the wrapping. A leper.

For an extra moment, Daddy gazes into the darkness in the hood, hoping against hope to make out the outline of his brother's face and a look of compassion that has never before been possible amid the sibling competition that they never outgrew. For another moment, Daddy wants to speak into the listening darkness and make his brother understand why he followed the stranger from Nazareth, where the teacher's feet had taken him, and how the teacher's words made all things new. But Daddy also knows that, unless he keeps silent, he cannot return to the simplicity of fishing for real fish and the peace of reigning over his own family. So he narrows his eyelids and takes a long drag from his cigarette and puffs out his answer to the leper, "Save your sympathy for a true disciple, and don't be so sure of your vision in the dark. I am just a fisherman."

The crowd begins to disperse amid scattered mutterings that Daddy is a liar or a coward or that he only played a bit part in the Galilean's show anyway. As the crowd thins out, Daddy looks down and sees two little ones who were hidden in the mass of adult bodies, two ragged, dusty waifs, Daddy's Suzy and Johnny looking up at him wide-eyed and perplexed as if he had just told them to hate their family. As he looks into their questioning eyes this time, he is not so quick with an answer, an appeasing explanation. All he knows is that he wants to go back to a life of fishing and never stop fishing. "What are you kids looking at? I'm not the guy these grown-ups think I am, some guy who rambled around the countryside with the man they threw in jail. I've got a home and kids a lot like you."

In the middle of the city, of all places, a cock crows. Daddy whirls around to see the misplaced cock, only to hear it louder again behind him. He whirls again, and now the cock is louder and closer behind him. He whirls again and again, the cock crowing louder, always out of sight, and just as Daddy is about to bolt down the street and out of the city, the cock's crow transforms into Mommy's voice, asking, "So what level of the animal kingdom have we descended to?" Daddy now searches wildly for her face, but she's always just outside of his peripheral vision. He searches the laughing faces of the crowd that reconvenes around him, madly scanning for some strange face or some shadowy figure, mouthing, "So what level of the animal kingdom have we descended to?" over and over into his ear and out of his sight.

"So what level of the animal kingdom have we descended to?" Daddy opens his mouth to call her name, but he is mute. "Wake up!" she booms, and Daddy struggles to get out of his skin, out of this dimension and into the dimension from which she calls. "Wake up!" Hands from nowhere shake him and his voice breaks out in a hollow shout.

"Wake up! You're dreaming!" she whispers a bit louder, and Daddy awakens, his heart beating like a bird's and his lungs racing to keep pace. "Where were you?" Daddy asks.

"I am right here," she replies with the tenderness of any woman when her husband has lapsed into childhood. She lays her head on his chest and holds him. "It was a bad nightmare, and it's over. You will be okay." Mommy is barely awake and may not remember this in the morning.

Daddy lets go of the tension in his face and neck and shoulders and trunk and legs and feet, one at a time as if to inventory his body to be sure it is all intact. With his left hand he lets go of the sheet, leaving a moist patch, and then he holds Mommy with both hands. He kisses the top of her head and stares into the darkness.

Dreams, like the darkness, do not solve problems. Dreams only accentuate them, filling our problems with all the emotion and meaning that we do not have time for while we wipe our children's tears and read them stories and check the locks. As Daddy stares into the darkness, he fancies no illusion that in the nightmare and the awakening there is some solution to the imperative problem of willingness to hate his family for Jesus' sake. He knows that something crucial is left undone, something he cannot put his finger on or explain away or check like a lock, but he knows that he must do something. Tomorrow he will get up early and eat his cereal and help get the children ready and go to work. He will come home and kiss his wife and play with the children and put them to bed and check the locks and kiss his wife again, but it won't be the same.

Daddy also knows that his heart is slowing for the night. His breathing is getting longer and deeper. He knows that it is grace that brought the nightmare and grace that brought his wife to awaken him. He knows that it is grace that brought those night prowlers to interrogate Peter, and grace that made him the Rock of his Teacher. It is grace that brought Jesus' rude interruption of Daddy's bedtime ritual, and grace that brings sleep.

And for love of Daddy and love of Mommy and love of Suzy and Johnny and for the love they have for one another, the God of grace will undo their family rituals and unlock their locks and do what is now undone.

CHAPTER 22

The Dance

Early in the morning he came again to the temple. All the people came to him and he sat down and began to teach them. The scribes and the Pharisees brought a woman who had been caught in adultery; and making her stand before all of them, they said to him, "Teacher, this woman was caught in the very act of committing adultery. Now in the law Moses commanded us to stone such women. Now what do you say?" They said this to test him, so that they might have some charge to bring against him. Jesus bent down and wrote with his finger on the ground. When they kept on questioning him, he straightened up and said to them, "Let anyone among you who is without sin be the first to throw a stone at her." And once again he bent down and wrote on the ground. When they heard it, they went away, one by one, beginning with the elders; and Jesus was left alone with the woman standing before him. Jesus straightened up and said to her, "Woman, where are they? Has no one condemned you?" She said, "No one, sir." And Jesus said, "Neither do I condemn you. Go your way, and from now on do not sin again."

John 8:2–11

It was midsummer, and already the morning sun in Jerusalem stirred the hot air thick, draining the earth of its water and the people of their spirits. Down the main street, a group of men swaggered, driving a woman like a farm animal with jabs and pushes, each man with a rock in his hand. Those closest to her seared her with their eyes and bit her with their words, and those taking up the rear laughed nervously at one another, announced their cause to passersby, and looked only half sure of what they were doing. These were righteous men, Pharisees and their apprentices, driven by a sweaty, angry justice.

They had found a man sleeping with this woman out of wedlock. He knew the law, the unofficial rules of the game, and how to confess and purify himself. But she was a woman, and all the helplessness and desperation of being a woman accused by men showed in her eyes and on her tear-stained face. Her hair was everywhere, and her bruises were everywhere. Through the mocking myriad of feet and faces, she saw Jesus, just another sweating man to her, and her life flashed before her eyes: Playing in the rain as a girl. The smell of her mother's stew. Inquiring and intense faces of men who visited her father one day. An October sunset.

At once her accusers spotted Jesus speaking to a small gathering in the Temple's outer courts, and together— without uttering a word—the Pharisees recognized an opportunity to dispose of two scoundrels while stoning one. If they merely asked Jesus to judge this case, they would put him in a catch-22: The Mosaic law clearly prescribed stoning as punishment for adultery. Most judges from their own group would hear these cases in private and revoke the offender's sentence. But here in public, in the shadow of the Temple, Jesus could either recommend stoning and appear harsh and legalistic or set her free and openly defy Mosaic law.

So they stopped rambling and shoving and spitting and walked toward him as erect and dignified as a college faculty at commencement, two holding her by each elbow, their countenance somber, with smugness thick in the cheeks beneath their steely eyes. They stopped her right in front of Jesus, her body bent and her legs faltering with fear, her head hung so that Jesus could see little more than a chaos of hair falling and flying in all directions. The man at her left elbow spoke for all of them, "Teacher, this woman was caught in the very act of committing adultery. Now in the law Moses commanded us to stone such women. Now what do you say?"

Jesus disarmed the righteous gang by moving his knees and his back and his index finger in a most unexpected gesture. He stooped. For an instant, every angry, righteous man there felt a wave of vindication as if their clever question literally brought Jesus to his knees. But their smug joy subsided as Jesus nonchalantly extended an index finger to the ground and started to write.

The gospel writer does not report what Jesus wrote, leaving us to wonder, as the righteous gang wondered, what was on Jesus' mind. Although the woman's accusers could see what he wrote, they probably did not know the meaning of it any more than we do. Some scholars speculate that Jesus wrote all the sins of each accuser, but such a list would have filled the dirt roads and dusty patches of Jerusalem. Besides, in a moment, Jesus would respond so elegantly that he did not need to belabor the point.

No, Jesus probably wrote something simple, something that at least distracted them, something that at most made their lives flash before their eyes. Perhaps he drew clouds and rain, a bowl of stew, the faces of strange and lonely men, a sunset—images an adulteress might recall before being stoned or images a Pharisee might recall before being judged.

Perhaps, on the other hand, Jesus wrote words. Since the men held stones intended to erase a life, he may have written words to remind the men and the woman of life: tremble . . . green . . . irony . . . kiss . . . salt . . . birth. Or since sin preoccupied the woman's accusers, he may have written words to remind them of sin: blame . . . walls . . . exploit . . . idol . . . smug . . . broken. Maybe Jesus wrote something much simpler, like a letter of the alphabet: A. A for adultery. Perhaps he wrote A in the powdery dust and waited for a few long moments while the hot summer morning breeze blew the A, the woman's sin, away.

When he finished writing in the dust, he arose slowly and looked into the eyes of the woman's righteous accusers. With eyes as calm and dark as the Dead Sea, he did not hurry to speak. As the men waited, they could feel the burden of the sun bearing down on their shoulders, the thick air closing in on their lungs. They felt their wet garments clinging to their skin. They saw his face—perhaps for the first time they saw his human face—another sweaty, tired face, but also a face with an unexpected look, a curious expression with hints of pity and bemusement. He glanced away for a moment, a long moment in which he could have muttered, "Father, forgive them; for they do not know what they are doing" (Luke 23:34). Instead he looked back at the men and said, very simply, "Let anyone among you who is without sin be the first to throw a stone at her." He caught the Pharisees in their own trap.

For the first time, Jesus saw the woman's eyes, saucer brown eyes looking at him from beneath a tempest of hair. She still trembled with fear because, as far as she knew, she was the only sinner there, and any moment she expected stones from the righteous gang to pelt her until every bone in her body broke. Although she was resigned to death, Jesus' writing and speaking disarmed her as well. Her life no longer flashed before her eyes. Her life stood in front of her with dust on his index finger and a peculiar compassion on his face.

Moments passed. She heard footsteps behind her. Jesus stooped again and began writing in the dust. She heard the thuds of stones dropping on the road, one by one. Before lifting her eyes, she knew that none of her accusers looked at her anymore. No man judged her now, except possibly this gentle and frightening one at her knees, drawing on the ground.

Whatever he wrote, he wrote especially for her. Possibly another reminder of the preciousness of life or another reminder of sin and the brokenness of life. Maybe he wrote another symbol for the sin for which she almost lost her life. He wrote what he wrote, and man and woman were still for a moment, listening as the footsteps behind her faded into the distance, watching as the hot wind blew the symbol of life or sin or her sin away.

Slowly he rose and looked into her eyes. They were alone now. Playing dumb, Jesus asked, "Woman, where are they? Has no one condemned you?" Just then she knew that she would live and that this man was her judge and that life and death would never again be the same. So she answered him, "No one, sir." His jaw tightened, but his eyes betrayed the smile that he fought back. In the shadow of the Temple, their bodies still, the judge stood tall, the defendant slightly bent; but their souls danced like two teenagers at a rock concert.

Jesus said, "Neither do I condemn you. Go your way, and from now on do not sin again." She stood waiting for a moment, hoping to dance in the street with him, but she looked away and turned and walked. At first she took slow, labored steps as her death flashed before her eyes: The angry faces. The sweat. The heat. The pushes and jabs. The man writing in the dust. Her pace quickened, and her steps began to spring slightly. She looked straight ahead toward home, through the streets and faces and structures that formed the setting and context of the life she almost lost. She did not look back at him, but she knew the day would come when she would dance with him in the shadow of the Temple.

CHAPTER 23

Independence Day

Then Jesus said to the Jews who had believed in him, "If you continue in my word, you are truly my disciples; and you will know the truth, and the truth will make you free." They answered him, "We are descendants of Abraham and have never been slaves to anyone. What do you mean by saying, 'You will be made free'?"

Jesus answered them, "Very truly, I tell you, everyone who commits sin is a slave to sin. The slave does not have a permanent place in the household; the son has a place there forever. So if the Son makes you free, you will be free indeed."

John 8:31–36

On the Fourth of July, the humidity rises high, and so does the sun. Lakes teem with sails, while on the shores, glistening sunbathers brown with radios blaring. Highways whir and rumble with bumper-to-bumper cars laughing at the speed limit. By day a thousand cans of beer and soft drinks pop open each second. By dusk bands perform, and children with mustard stains on their cheeks dart about playing tree tag like squirrels. By night the fireworks blaze with reds, whites, and blues, thundering and glittering like an apocalypse in the heavens.

These sights and sounds of Independence Day are not only the stuff of celebration but the very stuff that we celebrate. For many Americans, independence need not mean anything more abstract than driving like the wind, lolling by the surf, or seeing the entranced eyes of a slack-jawed child watching a fireworks show. Independence *is* the celebration itself, *is* the band playing, the speedboat pulling the trick skier, the sky diver touching down thirty yards from a hot dog vendor. "Only in America," a balding, middle-aged man in a T-shirt proclaims between belts of an Old Milwaukee. "Nothing like this in Russia or China." To him, as to many more, the sights and sounds of the Fourth of July *are* life, liberty, and the pursuit of happiness in living color.

In our more reflective moods, we think of independence as freedom of choice: Freedom to go to whatever church I please or no church at all. Freedom to speak my mind or not speak at all. Freedom to pursue my dreams, however simple or adventurous. Freedom to multiply my talents and gifts or bury my one talent in the backyard. Freedom to be wise or foolish or a wise fool. Independence adds up to all of our freedoms to do or say or feel as we choose, but on Independence Day, the people celebrate independence as something more than the sum total of our freedoms. Independence is, somehow, everything that makes us feel alive, everything we are willing to make joyous fools of ourselves for or to die for.

Although we have much to cherish, much freedom to be drunk with joy over on Independence Day, we also celebrate as a hungry people, a people not yet and perhaps never to be satisfied. America, like Israel, was founded in a moment of liberation, of shaking free of an oppressor to make a home in the homeland, and liberation and settling in the homeland did not offer and still does not offer the final answer to our longing, our searching, our hungering. Hunger characterizes us as much as freedom because freedom can never finish the job of satisfying us.

Freedom soars into the night sky with a mighty swish, building our anticipation, and exploding once, twice, three times in red, white, and blue, projecting tiny beacons in all directions until they hover and casually fall, extinguishing, leaving us again with the darkness of night. We can light up the sky with freedom time and time again, and always the conclusion is night, as surely as the conclusion of our lives is death. Freedom gives us light and dazzles us with life. But freedom passes away like fireworks, like life itself, and when the night forms the only background, freedom soon disintegrates in dying sparks and fluttering ashes, leaving only darkness.

Few in the crowd at the city park on Independence Day evening would want to hear that freedom is as short-lived and self-consuming as popping flickers of light in the sky. A young mother stares into the stars beyond the fireworks and with a look of longing whispers to no one in particular, "Is this all there is?" as her two boys exclaim over the bombs bursting in air and her husband discusses golf with a neighbor. A twelve-year-old boy stands alone wondering why he stands alone. The balding, middle-aged man in the lounge chair who earlier proclaimed, "Only in America," has now quietly consumed so much Old Milwaukee that he does not know where he is. Teenage girls in tight jeans flirt with boys discussing their favorite gin as a convertible blaring heavy metal music cruises by. This celebration is not darkness, but it may be a flickering of the dying light of freedom before darkness prevails.

These celebrators hunger for something that can last longer than freedom or for something on which freedom can light and brightly burn forever. Freedom begins a search, an adventure called life, and it is not the final answer. Freedom is, in the end, a hunger and not a satisfaction.

Hunger makes us restless. Worse, hunger makes us sell ourselves to the things we hunger for: wealth, power, prestige, sex, alcohol, a quick fix, an ideal love. If we honestly celebrate our freedom, we celebrate that for which we hunger, that to which we submit, that to which we sacrifice our freedom. Maybe that's why Independence Day speeches say so much about wealth and power, why Independence Day advertisements feature so much sex and alcohol, why quick fixes and ideal loves fill up Independence Day dreams by the shining sea.

There is no freedom in the end, only slavery to the things we hunger for, unless in our hungering restlessness, we somehow come across someone to sell ourselves to who gives back freedom in return. "If you continue in my word, you are truly my disciples; and you will know the truth, and the truth will make you free." Jesus blurted this out to a group of proud citizens who were so puffed up over being descendants of the father of their country that their citizenship had become a self-imposed slavery—something they could not see past. The freedom he offered flew in the face of the freedom they celebrated, so by the time he finished talking, they ran him out of the park as, I suspect, we might if he so rudely interrupted our fireworks show.

What offensive freedom did Jesus stir folks up with while the brass band took a break and things quieted down just enough for folks to hear him? Not Israelite freedom or American freedom. Not freedom of choice or freedom of speech or even freedom of religion. It was freedom born of obedience. It was freedom to follow a word told, not by a senator or therapist or CEO, but by a carpenter from the backwoods, a stranger who hangs out with loose women and party animals, a radical with dust in his hair and circles under his eyes. "The truth will make you free" meant that the scoundrel who pooped the freedom party gets the last word, is the Last Word, is the Truth that sets us free.

"God bless America," we sing even after we kick him out of the park, not realizing the subversiveness of the lyrics. The song presupposes that our hunger for idols and addictions will not bless us, but God's hunger for our hearts will. In other words, the song assumes that God's freedom, not ours, is the freedom that counts in the end. God asserted freedom from the day the Spirit hovered over the face of the deep and said, "Let there be light," until the day the Father kicked the stone away from the Son's tomb and laughed in the face of death. God keeps laughing because on that day our hungry freedom to live a lie died and freedom for us to live in truth claimed a permanent, Christ-shaped place in our souls.

Christian freedom is freedom from gods who, in the last analysis, are not free themselves, gods who cower in the face of death. Christian freedom means giving oneself over not to a God who dies and leads us to death as the final word, but who lives and leads us to life as the Final Word. This God does not respond to our commitment by addicting us to more, more, more, but by breathing into our nostrils the one free Spirit, giving us new life until everything that makes us feel alive, everything we are willing to make joyous fools of ourselves for or die for comes down to Christ, the one who set us free from death itself.

Easter, the day when we celebrate Christ's conquest of death, is our true independence day, and the Fourth of July is, at best, an anticipation of Easter. The Fourth comes with all the heat, noise, fireworks, and intoxication that hunger affords. Easter comes in the cool, misty stillness of dawn, bathing us in a morning light that drives out all darkness in the smiling aftermath of God's sassy laughter.

CHAPTER 24

Creation, Stillness, and Time

I consider that the sufferings of this present time are not worth comparing with the glory about to be revealed to us. For the creation waits with eager longing for the revealing of the children of God; for the creation was subjected to futility, not of its own will but by the will of the one who subjected it, in hope that the creation itself will be set free from its bondage to decay and will obtain the freedom of the glory of the children of God. We know that the whole creation has been groaning in labor pains until now; and not only the creation, but we ourselves, who have the first fruits of the Spirit, groan inwardly while we wait for adoption, the redemption of our bodies. For in hope we were saved.

Romans 8:18–24

When I was a boy, my family took some early summer jaunts in the mountains of North Carolina and Virginia. My father routinely drove like a fugitive pursued by helicopters and police cars in an eleventh-hour run for the border. Mother quietly agonized, gasping at the ugly face of certain death as Dad passed cars rounding mountain turns or tailgated 18-wheelers practically free-falling down steep highway slopes in fresh rain. My parents rode in the front seat, the anxiety seat, the seat for those old enough to know the power and perils of driving.

But in the back seat, we children sat safely removed from such concerns. We could see the windshield, yes, but images of oncoming traffic, skid marks, and broken guardrails amounted to little more than another television show, a high-speed fiction. Each of us practiced arts of distraction, our own ingenious strategies for ignoring the threat of calamity. In pensive silence my older brother observed my parents, undoubtedly psychoanalyzing them with precision which I, at the tender age of ten, could not yet appreciate. My younger sister slept the gentle sleep of one who inherited the serenity gene that our one-hundred-year-old grandmother reserved for her daughter's daughter.

I, too, found my talent for oblivion on those long mountain drives. This was not just a ride in the car, I thought. This was an adventure. We careened along the face of a lost planet, pressed in a chamber of vinyl, chrome, plastic, and glass, our vehicle powered by a tangle of metal and rubber that barely contained the explosions of igniting gasoline. I pressed my face to the window and watched the great stillness of creation. I could see valleys as God must see them, carpeted with green trees, and beneath the trees, there was life—lizard life and blackberry life and crow life and crawdad life and even human life. Green was life, and green was everywhere, palpable and quivering, suckling the earth, reaching toward heaven's cascading light. Clouds billowed and hovered, weightless as wisdom, and through the clouds, the blueness of eternity extended forever.

Suddenly the earth out my window ascended in a steep slope, and I faced a dark, chiseled wall of stone—the earth's crust. Years before, dynamite blasts literally carved through Mother Earth, making way for our car to cruise through her peaks without so much as a bump. For a moment we rushed headlong into the shadow of the rocky underworld.

In that moment I could see back in time for thousands upon millions of years. The wall of Earth's crust exposed layers of geological strata each of which required untold ages to develop. Each layer of earth laid bare on that mountain highway was the product of countless cycles of birth and death and decay and birth again, ashes to ashes, dust to dust, accumulating until the very face of the planet transformed. Fantastic species of flying giants, lumbering reptiles, and dreaming primates thrived for near eternities, only to die off and become extinct in environmental revolutions brought about by the throes of Earth giving birth to herself. As the planet groaned, faults shifted, glaciers migrated, molten rock erupted from Earth's seething core. For a momentary millennium, mother earth froze as if deserted by the sun, and in another fleeting millennium, she thawed and flushed, always in the pangs of giving birth. She still gives birth, warming even now to a fever pitch, burying dying species, shifting her crust, and entombing cities in lava and ash. It will make for a new layer of earth thousands, perhaps millions of years from now intermingled with the tar of this road, the metal and glass of this car, and fossils of our bones.

Our family car barreled past this artifact of time beyond recorded time, this dark citadel of ages past, in scarcely the time it takes to breathe one breath. We took more notice of billboards advertising truck stops, smoked turkeys, and family inns. I soon forgot my glimpse into the depths of time. My father heedlessly persevered as my mother silently fretted, and I watched the great stillness of creation hurtle by.

Creation. Stillness. Time. We come to know God in the immensity of these things. The priests who wrote the creation story (Gen. 1:1–2:4) saw God in the creation of light and darkness, sea and land, earth and stars, flying birds and creeping creatures, man and woman. Elijah, fleeing in despair from Jezebel's threats, heard God's voice in the stillness of Mount Horeb (1 Kings 19:8–13). God's disclosure in the expanses of time entranced the apostle John, who began his writings, "In the beginning was the Word, and the Word was with God, and the Word was God" (John 1:1), and he concluded his writings with the book of Revelation, the story of the thunderous culmination of all history, of all time in the final coming of Christ. But God also chooses to be known by little ones gazing out the window of a speeding vehicle as they watch the stillness of creation and the immensity of time fall behind them in a mad dash.

"Our God, our help in ages past, Our hope for years to come." We have sung these words more times than we can count in a transitory place we call church, in a flicker of time we call worship, acknowledging that the God beyond all creation, stillness, and time stands with us here and now at the crossroads of memory and anticipation, birth and death. As a child, I mastered the arts of distraction and practiced them as well when singing in church as when riding in the family car through the mountains. So it took me thirty-two years to hear the words of that hymn, but several Sundays ago I finally heard them: "A thousand ages in Thy sight Are like an evening gone; Short as the watch that ends the night Before the rising sun." I remembered the thousand ages I saw in the earth's crust rising by the highway, how I could only glance at those thousand ages because I was so small, and they were so great. God sees the thousand ages in a glance because they are so small, and God is so great.

"Time, like an ever-rolling stream, Soon bears us all away; We fly forgotten, as a dream Dies at the opening day." That is why my father drove so fast and furiously, why we all drive fast and furiously; because with each tick of the clock, with each groan of creation, we draw that much closer to the day when we are forgotten, when time bears us away, encased in a lower geological stratum. Yet we do not conclude with this verse, not because we refuse to face our destiny, but because God refuses to make death the final word.

"Our God, our help in ages past, Our hope for years to come, Be Thou our guard while life shall last, And our eternal home." The God who appears in deep stillness enters into the stirring of our lives, into our cars careening across the face of the planet, into our anxieties, hopes, and dreams, into the pain and joy of our relationships, and into the emptiness of our lonely moments with our faces pressed to a window. The God who created the universe with a Word becomes a created one, born on a cold night under the stars to a teenage mother, subject to the throes of creation's travail, subject to death. The God above and beyond all time enters into time. The God for whom all time is but a moment enters into the mere moments of our lives, into unexpected moments: A journey down a winding road. A view of a green valley. A visit to an empty tomb. By entering into the mere moments of our lives, God makes this earth, in spite of its labor and futility, its birth and decay, our home, but not our final home. Rather, God gives us an eternal home in Christ.